The Buildmeister's Guide

Achieving Agile Software Delivery

The Buildmeister's Guide

Achieving Agile Software Delivery

Kevin A. Lee

Second Edition

Copyright

ISBN 978-1-84728-373-3

About the Author

Kevin A. Lee has over 15 years of experience in implementing software build and release processes on projects of various sizes. He currently works as a Senior Technical Consultant specialising in Java Development, Application Lifecycle Management and Enterprise Integration. Kevin has worked as a consultant for Rational Software and IBM Software Services, helping customers in the adoption of new tools and processes. He has also held various development roles at large telecommunications and financial services organizations.

Kevin is the author of a number of books on the build process including *ClearCase, Ant and CruiseControl – The Java Developer's Guide to Accelerating and Automating the Build Process* and *Apache Ant - The Buildmeister's Guide*. He is also the author of many other articles and tutorials that have been published on the Internet. He contributes to open source projects such as Apache Ant and CruiseControl, and maintains a web portal dedicated to the build process (www.buildmeister.com).

Kevin holds a BSc. in computer science from the University of East Anglia (UEA) and is based in the UK; where he lives with his family in the Buckinghamshire countryside. Kevin can be contacted at: **kevin.lee@buildmeister.com**

For my ever loving wife and family – bless you as always.

Table of Contents

Preface

This preface first discusses my motivations, reasons and experience for writing this book. I then describe the framework of the book and how best to read it depending on your role, interests and experience.

Why this book came about

I have been working with software build and release processes for many years – either directly on projects or in a consulting capacity. I have certainly learnt many things, from experiences both good and bad, and from the many excellent people that I have worked with. I have never been someone who keeps information to themselves; rather I have always enjoyed structuring my ideas, experiences and opinions and writing them down.

In order to "giveback" some of this information, over the last few years I have been publishing material on *The Buildmeister* portal (www.buildmeister.com) – a community website I founded dedicated to discussing topics related to the build process. For those of you that don't already know, a *Buildmeister* (or Buildmaster) is the name for the individual who is tasked with defining and implementing the technical build process for a project.

The Buildmeister website has been well received, with many subscribers and participants. Although there is now a significant amount of information on this site, I would be the first to admit that it is not always as consumable and as easy to reference as you might want it to be. To help solve this, I decided to collect together some of the more significant content, combine it with some new unpublished information and publish the consolidated manuscript which you are now reading.

The purpose of this book

The purpose of this book is to research and document exactly what the build process is, and try to raise the level and quality of discussion that occurs about it. In the book I will look at how the build process affects and is affected by different styles of software development languages and methods and what intrinsic value a "well defined" build process actually brings to an organization. Don't worry I will take some time to described what I believe a "well defined" build process actually is. I will also break down the architecture and implementation of build processes and describes some patterns and techniques to ensure better implementation. Although, the book focuses on the build process in general, it does include some technical content where applicable – particularly on the implementation of build scripting and build control tools.

In this second edition I have rewritten and enhanced a significant proportion of the material. In particular I have added content related to describing what I call **Agile Software Delivery** and how it can be applied. From the feedback that I received on the first edition, I have decided to add more technical content – it seems Buildmeister's are inevitably technical people thirsting for knowledge! Finally, I have also expanded the sections on architecting and implementing build processes and tools with new ideas and patterns. Hopefully, I have also made the book more consistent and readable, concentrating on fundamentally important ideas and expanding on their implementation.

What this book covers

This book describes the build process and how to define and implement it as follows:

Chapter 1, "Introduction"

This chapter introduces why software is "built" and what a build constitutes. It discusses the benefits and value that a well defined build process can bring to an organization and also introduces the concept of Agile Software Delivery.

Chapter 2, "Build Process Definitions"

Definitions are important – they give us a framework for discussion. In this chapter I will define in detail a number of different aspects of the build process so that they can be used as a framework for the rest of the book.

Chapter 3, "Build Process Environments – Development Languages"

Any build process will be dependent on the environment that it is implemented in. In this chapter, I will look at how build processes and tools are typically implemented for a number of popular development languages.

Chapter 4, "Build Process Environments – Development Methods"

In addition to being affected by specific development languages, any build process will also be affected by a project's chosen development method. Similarly, it can also be affected by the vertical industry that the organization is operating in. In this chapter, I will look at a number of popular development methods and describe what requirements of the build process they make.

Chapter 5, "Build Process Core Skills"

In order to implement any build process you will need a good grounding in software development basics. You do not need to be an expert in everything – except maybe build scripting tools - but you will need certainly to possess some fundamental and core skills. In this chapter I will discuss the set of core skills that I believe every Buildmeister should possess a working knowledge of.

Chapter 6, "Architecting your Build Process"

When implementing any build process, it is important to understand what you want to achieve. This chapter introduces a high-level capability architecture for a typical build process and looks at the scope, decisions and issues that you should be aware of before implementation.

Chapter 7, "Implementing your Build Process"

At some stage you will either need to physically implement a new build process or refine an existing one. This chapter describes a number of patterns and techniques for implementing a build process.

Chapter 8, "Epilogue"

In the final chapter I discuss how best to use the information contained within this book and elsewhere to start making the changes to your own build process.

How to read this book

This book is not just for Buildmeisters. It is intended to be high-level and readable by many different members of the software development team. For different roles I would recommend the following:

- Managers and team leads would be best served by reading chapters 1 to 4 as this will provide an understanding of what the build process is and why I believe it is so important.

- Developers and architects should read chapters 1 to 4 and chapter 6 as this will enable them to understand some of the ways that build processes are best implemented.

- Finally, Buildmeisters should obviously read the whole of the book – maybe even several times!

Note that in the course of the book I discuss the implementation of the build process for a number of different environments – development languages and methods. It might be that you are implementing your build process in only one of these environments. In this case feel free to skip over any unrelated content.

CHAPTER 1

Introduction

Everything has been said before, but since nobody listens we have to keep going back and beginning all over again.

Andre Gide

This chapter introduces why software is "built" and what a build constitutes. It discusses the benefits and value that a well defined build process can bring to an organization and also introduces the concept of Agile Software Delivery.

Why build?

Anyone who has worked on a software development project will be familiar with the term "build". Even for a complete software novice, it would not take much imagination to guess what the term refers to. Everyone has "built" something at some time in their life - maybe a Lego dinosaur, a dog kennel or even for the really adventurous an entire house! Of course, what is being referred to in these three examples is the construction of something that has an observable and tangible result – the same can't always be said of software builds.

One of the main differences with a software build is that it doesn't necessarily have to resolve to a finished product. The build might fail, the process to create it might not finish, yet in some ways such failures are often seen as successes - as they have uncovered something that is wrong and can hopefully be fixed. Try applying that same concept to the construction industry - you've built the dog kennel but the dog can't fit in it, you've built a house but forgot the windows! In these circumstances you wouldn't get a second chance and probably be recommended to look for another job or take up another hobby pretty quickly. The obvious question is: **why is building software so different?**

What we are really dealing with here is the recognized limitations of the software engineering industry - software as art, as an evolving and moving target. In software development we don't necessarily have a complete blue-print and neither do we know all the answers up front. We would therefore like something to visualize - to be able to demonstrate and talk about - as we try and find our way there. If we could develop software correctly - the first time - then we would only ever need to create a single build, upon whose completion our job would be done.

As we live in the real world however and recognize our industries limitations, we understand that we will never get things right the first time. We are dealing with people, potentially many of whom are working on the same project. They might have slightly different opinions about what the end result should be, they might even make mistakes - they're human after all! What we need are regular milestones or integration points, where we can bring together all the individual pieces of work that have been created so far. This will allow us to correct those mistakes and consolidate those opinions. In software development this is the real reason we create builds.

Building versus Compilation

You will have noticed that nowhere in the previous section did I mention compilation. Some people often use the phrases building and compilation interchangeably. However, I believe it is important to understand that the two are different. Compilation should be seen as one part of an overall build process and not the end result. In fact some popular interpreted languages such as Perl, Python or Ruby require no direct compilation process; however they still need an overriding build process. In chapter 2, I will discuss in detail a set of "functions" that a build process can encompass.

The value of the build process

The first thing that anyone working in software development should remember – no matter what level you work at – is that you have a customer and a set of constraints within which you must work. No matter how fun it is developing software, there is usually a specific environment in which you must operate. There is also usually someone paying you for your time – no matter however indirect it is. Implementing a build process is no different, your constraints will be the software development environment in which you are operating and your customer will be different people at different times: from developers to testers to project management and finally to the end users.

Developers are an obvious first key customer for the process. As I discussed at the beginning of this chapter, the larger the project and the more developers you have on it, the more you need some mechanism to pull these tasks together - to identify a common baseline for ongoing development and to demonstrate the progress that has been made so far. This is usually encapsulated in an "integration build" process and in which most software development teams see significant value. For me however, a well defined build process can have value at a number of different levels:

- **To the individual developer** - where the value is the confidence that their incremental changes can be successfully incorporated into the team environment.
- **To the project and/or team** - where the value is being able to uncover integration issues between different developer's changes.
- **For the organization as a whole** - where value is the demonstration of executable progress together with any resultant metrics, as well as the potential savings through knowledge and implementation re-use and sharing.

A well defined build process can be the heartbeat of a successful project. I believe most people do not spend enough time early in their development lifecycle considering how often they should build, what they should build and what the overall functions of the build process should be. Proactively assessing this is what I call finding your "project rhythm" and which I discuss in detail in chapter 6.

As well as being a facilitator of integration and communication, a well defined build process can also demonstrate significant value by helping to achieve organizational business drivers. If you have read any recent publications or literature on the state of the commercial software development industry, you will no doubt be aware that the industry is fundamentally shaped by its requirement to meet organizational businesses drivers such as:

- **Regulatory Compliance and Governance**
- **Globalization and Outsourcing**

- **Time to Market and Quality**

At the technical level, I believe these business drivers can usually be met by addressing the following key software development challenges:

- **Traceability and Completeness** – knowing throughout the complete software development lifecycle why you are doing what you are doing and that it contains all of what you intended.

- **Repeatability and Reliability** - being able to do the same thing over and over again and it being correct each time.

- **Agility and Speed** - having a process in which changes can be integrated quickly or as and when needed and that completes in as short a time as possible.

If you think about each of these challenges for a minute, you would hopefully come to the same conclusion as me in that a well defined build process can go a significant way in helping to achieve them. A build process can help with traceability by automatically capturing and reporting on the changes (new features, defects and so on) that have gone into the build. Information such as this is critical for the consumers of the builds. For example, the test team will need to know which of the defects they raised have been included in the build; similarly the audit team might need to know that only the changes that were proposed to be implemented, actually have been and nothing else has "sneaked in".

A build process can help with repeatability and reliability by creating a snapshot of everything at the moment it is created, including source file versions, compiler settings and the operating system environment itself. This information is critical for being able to reproduce an environment for fixing defects after a product has been released.

Finally, a build process can help with agility and speed by being able to be setup and executed quickly so as to meet the needs of its users. It should also be capable of being executed continually - maybe many times a day. This capability is critical for delivering hot-fixes quickly but also for projects practicing Continuous Integration [FowlerCI] where developers are working on small incremental changes and integrating them frequently.

Build and Release Management

One of the terms that is often used to describe the implementation of the build process is "Build and Release Management". Everything that build and release management encompasses (at least in the software sense) is covered in this book. The concern I always have with this term is it used in different contexts, for example, Release Management is also used in a much wider sense (typically as specified by the IT Infrastructure Library – www.itil.co.uk). In such a context, Release Management also includes project- or program-related issues such as how to manage and assess the impact of defects against multiple release streams, as well as planning the rollout of complete software, hardware and communications infrastructures. In this book I will use the term **build process** for the mechanistic construction of the build - and **deployment** – for the process of *releasing* and deploying its outputs.

Agile Software Delivery

When I talk with different people about the build process, they typically visualize a very narrow definition – usually thinking in terms of code, of compilation, and of the technical implementation of build tools. These are some of the aspects of a build process but certainly not all. Since I believe, the build process is a fundamental enabler for a complete Application Lifecycle Management (ALM) solution; I often prefer to talk about the build process as enabling **software delivery**.

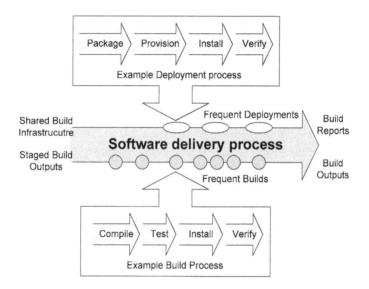

Figure 1 – Agile Software Delivery

To me, software delivery is a mechanistic foundation. It is not a process or method in its own right, rather it is a collection of automated functions to underpin ALM and help bridge the delivery gap that exists between development teams, operations and end users. By using this definition, it is hopefully clearer that the build process is not about building for building's sake – a build has no value in isolation – rather it is about helping to add value to a project – incrementally, over time, and throughout its entire lifecycle.

In addition to this definition, I also believe that software delivery should be as *agile* as possible. This is not agile as in the sense of Agile

Development practices[1]; rather it is the need for agility in processes that can potentially be executed many times over and that need to share and publish relevant information as a continuous pipeline. Figure 1 illustrates my visualization of the pipeline concept of **Agile Software Delivery** - with frequent and repeatable builds and deployments. It illustrates that shared infrastructure and the outputs of previous (related) builds can be used as inputs to the software delivery process. The idea behind this is the more that can be shared the more likely it is possible to decrease the total build time and to ensure consistency. It also illustrates that the outputs of the software delivery process are the build outputs and builds reports, which are made available so that content can be potentially shared by other processes.

In order to implement a build process to enable Agile Software Delivery I believe there are three key enablers:

- **Automation** – of manual and repetitive tasks in as quick and timely a way of possible.
- **Communication** – of build success or failure as well as reports and metrics on build content, trends and quality.
- **Re-use** – of build tools, technology and infrastructure across project and organizational boundaries.

Enablers such as these are often easy to state but hard to implement. In the course of this book I will therefore describe them in more detail as well as discuss strategies on how they can be successfully implemented. Hopefully by doing so, you will then be able to achieve Agile Software Delivery in your own environment.

---

[1] Although I believe implementing specific Agile Development practices such as Continuous Integration and Testing can significantly help to achieve Agile Software Delivery.

Summary

As you will have noticed, I place a tremendous amount of significance and value on the build process, both as an integration and communication mechanism as well as a fundamental business enabler. I believe a well defined build process can contribute significantly to the success of a project. Therefore the value it can bring in terms of visibility and incremental, demonstrable progress should not be underestimated.

I have made reference a number of times in this section to a "well defined" build process. In order to bring some clarity to what such a process could include, in the next chapter I will next spend some time defining exactly what I believe the build process is in detail.

CHAPTER 2

Build Process Definitions

Just definitions either prevent or put an end to a dispute.
Nathaniel Emmons

Definitions are important – they give us a framework for discussion. In this chapter I will define in detail a number of different aspects of the build process so that they can be used as a framework for the rest of the book.

Profiles

Every software development project involves some form of build, from the one man "helloworld.exe" to the 500 developer, multiple team missile control system. The exact form that the build takes will depend on a number of factors such as the chosen development language, the operating system environment or the development methodology; however there are generally three profiles of builds that you might want to carry out and that are illustrated in Figure 2.

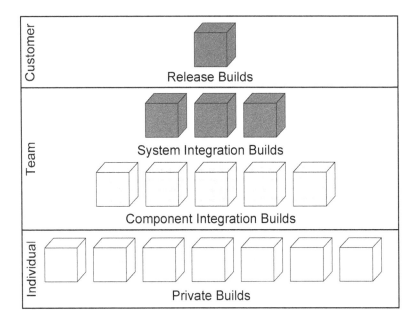

Figure 2 - Build Profiles

These profiles are variations on the profiles that were first defined in Berczuk and Appleton's book *Software Configuration Management Patterns* [Berczuk02], and their additional paper with Konieczka, *Build Management for an Agile Team* [BerczukBM]. In more detail, these three profiles can be defined as follows:

Private Build

A Private Build refers to a build that is created by a developer in his or her own workspace. This type of build is usually created for the purpose of verifying the ongoing status of the developer's changes, i.e., to assess whether his or her source code compiles.

Integration Build

An Integration Build is a build that is carried out by an assigned integrator or central function. This type of build can be carried out manually by a lead developer or a member of the build team, or alternately via an automatically scheduled program or service. This build is created to assess the effect of integrating a set of changes across a development team.

There can be multiple types of Integration Builds especially for large systems. Figure 2 illustrates builds at both the component and system level (where all the components are rebuilt or consumed).

Release Build

A Release Build is a build that is carried out by a central function, usually a member of the build team. This build is created with the express intention of being delivered to a customer - either internal or external. A Release Build is also usually created in an isolated and controlled environment.

One important point to note is that although there are three explicit profiles defined here, it does not mean that each type of build should be constructed in an entirely different manner. In fact, I would expect and recommend that the same set of build scripts be utilized, irrespective of by whom and for what reason the build is being carried out. Using a single set of build scripts will ensure that any errors with the build scripts are identified at an early stage – during development or integration time - not when you are just about to make a release.

One question that I frequently get asked is: if the same build scripts are being executed each time, is a Release Build really necessary? The answer to this is potentially no – but it depends on what you define your Release Build process to be. From a process point of view, there are typically additional activities that you will need to go through when creating a release. These can include writing or collating documentation, creating distribution media, archiving and so on. There might also be specific deployment activities that are carried out as part of the Release Build, for example building and deploying to Acceptance Test environments[1]. A simple way[2] of thinking about the difference is that Integration Builds validate your progress whereas Release Builds validate your content and ability to deploy.

Pre-commit builds

One variation of the build profiles identified is the **pre-commit build**. This refers to a pseudo Integration Build carried out by a developer prior to them committing their changes into the repository. Such a build is intended to verify that the developer's changes would work in a more controlled environment (not just on their own desktop machine).

Usually, some form of tool support is required to carry out this type of build and hence it is not included as one of the standard build profiles. Also, if Integration Builds are carried out frequently (maybe several times a day), developer integration issues will be picked up quickly when the build fails and fixed. This often acts as a forcing function and ensures that developers take more care over what they are committing to the repository.

Functions

When most people think about the build process they usually think about compilation, however a build should be seen as an end-to-end

---

[1] I will discuss more about deployment environments in chapter 6.

[2] Perhaps overly simple, but it is good enough differentiator for our purposes.

process. Let us refer back to the analogy I made with house construction at the beginning of chapter 1. If you were constructing a house you would not say you were finished when the bricks, timber and masonry had gone up. You would also have to fit electrics, plumbing, decorate the house and also have it surveyed and safety tested so that it was fit for purpose. These are all distinct functions in their own right. In a similar way the software build process can be broken down into the following functions:

Version Control

The Version Control function carries out activities such as workspace creation and updation, baselining and reporting. It creates an environment for the build process to run in and captures metadata about the inputs and outputs of the build process to ensure repeatability and reliability.

Static Analysis

The Static Analysis function is used to check that all developers have adhered to some basic coding standards and that language specific best practices have been implemented. The use of Static Analysis as part of the build process is a good way of ensuring that any code is changeable and readable by all members of the development team.

Static Analysis tools can be integrated into the build process to warn about potentially "undesirable" aspects such as code that is highly coupled or has a high cyclomatic complexity[3], code that has memory leaks, or even code that has been overly "copy-and-pasted".

---

[3] See www.sei.cmu.edu/str/descriptions/cyclomatic_body.html for a description of cyclomatic complexity

Compilation

The Compilation function turns source files into directly executable or intermediate objects. Not every project necessarily compiles code - some scripted languages can be executed directly - however the majority of projects still do. The important thing to note here is that Compilation is not the build process, just part of it.

Unit and Component Testing

The Unit Testing function is the first quality gate for the build. It is used to assess whether developer's changes work together at the code unit level. A build which passes all of its unit tests (if the tests are comprehensive and well written) has a good chance of being a quality build.

Component Testing is used to assess whether code units function correctly together. Where components are not available or need to be executed in a runtime environment, stubs or **mock objects** are typically used. A mock object is a simulated object, for example, a class to mimic a database when normal database access is not available.

Data Processing

The Data Processing function creates, parses or transforms data files into outputs. It is included here because not every build consists purely of code and tests. In some industries the compilation process is a very small part of the overall build process. For example, the multimedia games industry has time consuming build processes that include the generation of three dimensional graphics from models.

Packaging

The Packaging function takes the outputs of the build and bundles them together so as to be complete and installable.

These packages are sometimes referred to as distribution archives. In technical terms Packaging might mean bundling up a set of Java classes and libraries into an archive (a JAR or EAR file) so that it is available to be installed onto a server.

Functional Integration Testing (FIT)

The Functional Integration Testing[4] or Link Testing function is a secondary quality gate and is the execution of a small core subset of functional tests - usually against a deployed application. It is executed to give the test team confidence that the build is suitable for further testing.

Runtime Analysis

The Runtime Analysis function is typically executed as a "side affect" of the Unit Testing and/or FIT function. It can be used to verify aspects of system performance or test coverage[5]. For example Code Coverage metrics can be gathered to allows the project to assess how much of the total code base has been exercised and what areas of an application additional functional testing should concentrate on.

Deployment

The Deployment function transitions the build to its runtime environment. Builds are usually only automatically transitioned to immediately related environments, for example, Integration or System Test environments. Live or Production environments are sometimes deployed to automatically (as part of a secure, controlled Release Build process) but most of the

---

[4] I've also heard this called System Verification Testing but the point is that it is a subset of automated tests.

[5] Since collecting code coverage metrics can significantly impact performance, you should not gather performance and coverage metrics at the same time.

time this type of deployment is usually carried out manually – maybe as a distinct process in its own right – and by a separate team.

The Deployment function also includes provisioning the hardware and software on the target environment so that the build is installed correctly. I will discuss more about deployment in chapters 6 and 7.

This is not an exhaustive list nor should it be seen as a prescriptive list, however it illustrates that a well defined build process includes mechanistic (Compilation), quality (Static/Runtime Analysis, Unit Testing, Functional Integration Testing) and publishing (Packaging, Deployment) functions.

Is your build process RADICAL?

When designing any build process I try to make sure that any implementation is RADICAL. This is not radical as the dictionary defines it (although it is sometimes good to be radical), but an acronym which stands for a build process that is:

Reusable – it can (potentially) be used across multiple projects.

Accessible – it can be used by different members of the development team, e.g. Developers, Testers, Buildmeisters. Each of whom will probably have different entry points.

Documented – it can be understood by different members of the development team – at least at a high level.

Integrated – it is integrated with other development tools, including version control tools and IDEs.

Complete – it can build (and deploy) a complete project or application from beginning to end (and includes most of the build functions described in this section).

Automated – it can be executed automatically, with no (or at the most limited) manual intervention.

Lean – its implementation adds value to your project (and ultimately your business) as rapidly as possible.

Later on in this book I will describe implementation techniques to make your own build process RADICAL.

Infrastructure

In order to execute Integration or Release Builds you should always use dedicated and controlled servers. Although I have seen some small projects develop, build and release from a developer's workstation this is not a repeatable or auditable process and should be avoided. The typical infrastructure components that form a standard build infrastructure are as follows:

- **Developer Desktop** – not a server per se but a workstation on which developers implement changes and (typically) conduct their Private Builds. In some organizations developer desktops are typically nothing more than a dumb terminal and developers carry out a remote login to a shared machine where they edit, compile and debug.
- **Version Control Server** - a server on which code repositories are held and which developers commit their changes so that they are included in Integration or Release Builds.

- **Build Server** - a server on which Integration or Release Builds are conducted either manually or using an automation tool.

- **Test Server** - a server on which the outputs of the Integration or Release Builds are deployed to in order to assess the quality of the build and its suitability for further testing (see the FIT function above)

An example of how these different components are related is illustrated in Figure 3.

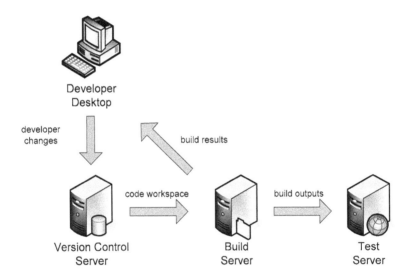

Figure 3 - Build Server Infrastructure

Developer Desktop builds are typically executed when some form of Integrated Development Environment (IDE) is being used, for example, Eclipse or Visual Studio.NET. IDEs typically have their own internal build functions to automatically compile and deploy to a developers own test environment. This can by very productive but should be re-enforced by Integration Builds so that machine specific errors are not introduced. Note that the amount of physical servers that are required will depend on the size, complexity and nature of your development environment. For example, if you are developing a product for many different platforms, e.g., Windows, Linux and UNIX, then you would implement different **Build Server Variants** for each platform. Similarly if your build process takes a significant amount of time to execute, then you would probably implement a **Build Server Farm** which consisted of a number of servers over which the overall build could be distributed.

As part of your build process you might also deploy to servers other than just a single Test Server. For example you might deploy to a Test Application Server (e.g. BEA Weblogic) and a Test Database Server (e.g. Oracle). In order to achieve Agile Software Delivery I believe that you should build and deploy to representative "production" runtime environments as early as possible. I will discuss this in more detail in chapters 6 and 7.

Roles

In chapter 1 I discussed some of the customers of the build process. Different "types" of users will be affected by your build process: from developers, to testers, to project management and your operations team. However there is a core set of user groups that will be more directly involved in the build process and that can be summarised as follows:

- **Developers** - the creators of source code, unit tests and supporting artefacts that are "built" as part of the build process.
- **Build Engineers (Buildmeisters)** - the creators of the build process itself (via tools and/or scripting), and who are responsible for either automating the

execution of the build process or for executing it themselves directly.

- **Deployment Engineers** - the creators of scripts to deploy or transition the output of the build process to their runtime environment. In large corporate organizations Deployment Engineers are often in a completely different group (IT Operations) to the development team.

Note, that these roles might have slightly different names in your own organization and also, that a single person could fulfil more than one role - the important thing is that the roles are carried out. An example of how these different roles can interact is illustrated in Figure 4.

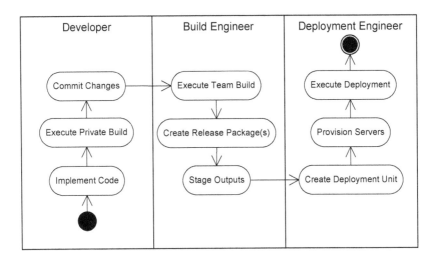

Figure 4 - Build Roles

In Figure 4 developers implement code and execute their own Private Builds. When they have tested their changes locally, they then commit their changes to the Version Control Server. At a pre-defined interval, the Build Engineer then builds the collective set of developer changes, creates an application release package from the results and stages (stores) it in some well known location ready to be installed. Finally, at some stage the Deployment Engineer picks up this output and defines a logical **Deployment Unit**[6] which consists of all the related software that they need to install. They then provision one or more servers using this information and finally deploy the release of the application onto them.

This interactive process might be slightly different in your own environment, but you should always try to identify your build roles and responsibilities early. For example, in some teams the Build Engineer role is completely automated and the scripts to achieve it are updated by developers as and when needed. In other teams - especially large-scale development projects - there might be a specific Build or Release Engineering team who are solely responsible for defining and executing Integration or Release Builds across many different projects.

Software Configuration Management and builds...

The term Software Configuration Management (SCM) is commonly used to refer to the process of managing and controlling all software development assets – including builds. It is differentiated from basic source code version control in that it supports the following four functional areas:

Version Management - Enables the secure and controlled storage, retrieval and versioning of all project assets (source code, documentation, test results and so on).

Change Management - Enables the capture, tracking and management of all types of project changes (requests for change, enhancements, defects) and direct comparison of these

---

[6] I will define the Deployment Unit in detail in chapter 6.

changes to the versions of the project's assets used to implement them.

Build Management - Enables the consistent and reliable construction (build) of software applications and reports on their contents and results.

Process Management - Enables the reporting of actions, history and milestones and provides the capability to customize or enforce development workflow and procedures.

As you can see from this definition the build process or Build Management is a core part of SCM. However, from what I have observed there are limited guidelines, documentation and material on exactly how best to implement Build Management. I believe that part of the reason for this is that the successful implementation of Build Management is ultimately technology dependent. Despite this however, there are still a large number of general good practices that can be applied to any build process (and which I will discuss in this book).

To implement any build process, at some stage you will need to drop down a level from the application of general Build Management processes and apply them to your own technology environment. This is another reason why I prefer to talk about the build and deployment process, as by my definition it includes the definition, implementation, execution and control of builds not just the management of them.

Integration and build patterns

Integration is one of the most important and often neglected aspects of software development. Essentially, integration combines separately developed components or subsystems so that problems in their interactions can be addressed. There are typically three integration strategies that can be adopted and these are summarized in the following section.

Milestone Integration

In Milestone Integration, software components are developed in isolation and then integrated at a specific milestone – perhaps as infrequently as once a month. Figure 5 illustrates Milestone Integration for two components which are integrated together for the first time at a specific point in time onto the **mainline**[7].

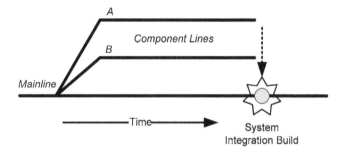

Figure 5 - Milestone Integration

Milestone Integration is often called **big-bang integration**; it is a high risk approach that can result in significant scrap and rework and should therefore be avoided.

---

[7] The codeline patterns are taken from [Berczuk02].

Continuous Integration

Continuous Integration is the opposite of Milestone Integration. In Continuous Integration, small development changes are integrated frequently (perhaps many times a day) directly onto the mainline. Figure 6 illustrates Continuous Integration with regular builds.

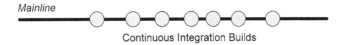

Continuous Integration Builds

Figure 6 - Continuous Integration

In practice, Continuous Integration is only practical if rigorous unit and component testing is implemented to validate small, incremental changes. If implemented successfully however it can reduce integration to a trivial exercise.

Integration in more detail...

Software integration can be trivial or complex. In general it follows a Develop-Build-Fix pattern to: develop some specific functionality, build it as part of a system, and fix the functionality if any problems are found.

System Integration looks at the complete system operating environment, for example integration with operating systems, third party components or external systems. In such cases integration typically involves deploying a built system and executing Functional Integration Tests to validate its fundamental operation.

Staged Integration

Staged Integration can be seen as a practical form of integration. Its aim is to integrate early and often but because of complexity it recognizes that this is not always possible. A typical example is after a product has been released. Development continues for the next release, but a number of problems are found in the field that need to be urgently fixed and delivered. To achieve this, short lived branches are created in the version control system and upon which the fixes are made.

If a collection of fixes is being made, as for example in a maintenance release, then this branch would effectively be a subproject in its own right. In such a case Continuous Integration could also be carried out for this subproject but on its own subproject codeline. When completed the subprojects are then integrated back onto the mainline via a System Integration Build. This process is illustrated in Figure 7.

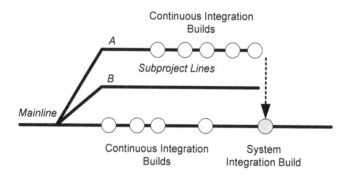

Figure 7 - Staged Integration

There can be other reasons for Staged Integration, for example "experimental" code development, however since Staged Integration is effectively promoting code isolation, care should be taken to ensure sure that such activities are short lived.

Integration at the binary level

As well as System Integration via version control baselines, it is also possible to integrate at the binary level for those environments that support it. For example in Java, a number of the components to be integrated could be pre-built Java archives. In this case Integration would then consist of selecting the complete set of binary versions and building against any custom developed code.

Binary component integration works well in principle but if there is a significant amount of version dependency information, then tool support that manages this metadata is often required. In Java, tools such as Apache Ivy and Apache Maven have mechanisms to support this approach.

Component Integration

Large-scale systems often consist of multiple components, the development of which are often a project in their own right and take significant time to develop. In such cases integration is desirable but difficult because of the potential interdependencies between components. To help solve this problem version control Component Integration baselines are often used to identify system level candidates and integration carried out.

Figure 8 illustrates two components being developed in isolation. Component *B* completes a set of activities first and makes available (delivers) baseline *B1*. This baseline (together with the recommended set of baselines from other components) is built as part of a System Integration Build and a system baseline *SYS1* created. This baseline is then recommended for use by all of the components. Component *A* subsequently rebases to this baseline, makes any required changes and delivers baseline *A2*. This baseline is then built in system baseline *SYS2*.

If components are well designed with loose coupling, then system integration is a relatively trivial exercise of selecting baselines, rebuilding and verifying their interoperation. Unfortunately, some systems are not as well designed and System Integration can be a complex exercise.

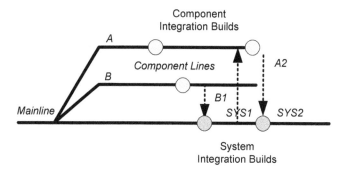

Figure 8 – Component Integration

To reduce integration issues, I believe that Component Integration should include frequent integration exercises (at least once a week) – even if functionality is partially complete. If not then it is effectively Milestone Integration with all of its inherent problems. Also, since the components are being developed as projects in their own right, there is no reason why they cannot use Continuous Integration on their own codeline.

Build frequencies

How often you decide to integrate will dictate to some degree how often you build. For example if you are carrying out Component Integration then you will need to build before delivery and after rebasing. However builds can also be carried out to validate ongoing changes. There are at least three standard and well known build frequencies that are used in software development. These can be summarised as follows:

- **The Weekly Build** – a mechanism typically used by large software development projects practising Component Integration. In this approach, changes from different teams are delivered and integrated into a System Integration Build once a week.

- **The Daily Build and Smoke Test** – a mechanism whereby an Integration Build is carried out once a day (usually overnight) based on all the changes that have been committed to the Vesrion Control Server. In addition a suite of "smoke" tests is run against it to check the validity of the build. This pattern was first publicized by Microsoft [McConnell96].

- **The Continuous Integration Build** – a mechanism whereby a version control repository is continuously monitored and an Integration Build is executed automatically when a developer commits a change to the repository. The pattern was first documented by Martin Fowler [FowlerCI] as part of an Agile development approach. It requires short build times (less than 10 minutes) and a comprehensive set of unit tests.

In general the more often you build, the more likelihood there is that you will uncover integration problems at an early stage. Therefore, I believe you should always endeavour to execute builds as frequently as you can.

Although most organizations recognize this basic premise it is still amazing that more do not carry out at least a Daily Build and Smoke

Test. This is usually because they do not know or communicate their develop and delivery rate and so it is hard to say the optimal frequency of when a build should be carried out. To be able to define which build schedule would be more appropriate you can start by discovering your "project rhythm". I will discuss how to achieve this in chapter 6.

Summary

The build process is all about ensuring that builds can be reliably constructed, their content controlled and their outputs deployed to test or run-time environments. By breaking down the build process in terms of individual functions and roles, as well as understanding the lifecycle of a typical build you can start to understand more about the scope of the build process and what a typical framework would be.

In the next chapter, I will make use of these definitions and look at how they might be applied in different development environments.

CHAPTER 3

Build Process Environments:

Development Languages

The purpose of most computer languages is to lengthen your resume by a word and a comma.
Larry Wall

Any build process will be dependent on the environment that it is implemented in. In this chapter, I will look at how build processes and tools are typically implemented for a number of popular development languages.

Development Languages

There a vast array of different development languages. It is not possible to discuss each of them and how they can be built. Instead I will concentrate on a number of well known and well used languages as follows:

- C and C++
- Java

- Microsoft .NET languages
- and interpreted languages in general

The first and most obvious comment to make is that the majority of development languages have their own preferred build scripting tool, for example C and C++ have Make, Java has Apache Ant or Apache Maven and Microsoft VS.NET has MSBuild or NAnt. Each of these tools has their own individual issues and nuances. As well as tool related issues, the development language that you work in can also affect the build process in other ways. For example, if the compiled output needs to be optimized then the compilation process can take a significant amount of time and techniques should be used to reduce the overall build time.

The aim of this chapter is therefore twofold: firstly it is to discuss how different development languages can impact the implementation of a build process, and secondly it is to introduce you to the most commonly used build tools for each language, providing an example of their use and discussing current issues with their implementation.

C and C++

C and C++ are both compiled languages, and are typically chosen for performance reasons. Compiled C and C++ code is usually fast and has a relatively small footprint. As a result, performance critical applications such as operating systems, telecommunications devices and multimedia applications are all traditionally written in C or C++. However, in order to benefit from quicker performance, C and C++ applications usually have to be fully optimized. This can lead to very long compilation times – ranging from several hours to maybe even several days[1]. Any build process implemented for a C or C++ application must therefore do everything it can to reduce the total build time, usually by distributing the build process so that it is executed on multiple servers. The build scripting language that is typically used for C and C++ applications is a variant of **Make**.

Overview of Make

Make is the original build scripting tool. Created by Stuart Feldman at Bell Labs as long ago as 1977, Make was developed to support dependency tracking and archiving for applications with large numbers of source files. It became popular very quickly and over time has been delivered with practically every BSD/UNIX operating system variant. Unfortunately, most vendors have also taken the opportunity to "enhance" Make for their own bespoke environments; consequently there is really no single, industry recognised implementation. Probably the most common however is **GNU Make** - an open source variant maintained by the GNU Project (www.gnu.org). It is therefore this variant of Make which we will be discussing in this section.

In its simplest form, Make can be used to create and coordinate a sequence of operating system scripts or commands. However, it is more typically used to help developers keep track of which files are needed to build a particular program or application and to sort out the dependency relationships between files; for example which source code files, header files and libraries make up a specific executable. Make helps implement a simple form of **build avoidance**, in that it looks at the date/time stamps of individual files, and the dependency relationships that you have defined, to work out what (if any) of the files from your complete application it needs to re-build.

---

[1] I once worked on a project that took 48 hours to compile when fully optimized. Needless to say we implemented aggressive parallel compilation and distribution techniques to bring this down to an "acceptable" level.

The input to Make is a textual file, by default called **makefile** or **Makefile** (although any filename can be used). A complete application can be built using one or many makefiles (which are commonly located at different component or directory levels). Each makefile describes a set of **targets**, which are the objects that can be made. Targets are usually the name of an executable or library but can also be the name of a specific "activity", for example "clean" or "release" - such targets are often called **phony** targets since they do not map to a physical file. By default, a target "exists" if it is present on disk (i.e., there is a file with that name).

Each target is constructed using a set of **commands** - which are usually calls to compilers, linkers, pre-processors and so on, but can actually be any operating system script or utility. A command or set of commands is executed by Make to bring a target up to date. Each target can also have **dependencies**. A dependency[2] is a relationship between a target and the other objects that are needed to construct it. For example, an executable depends on object files and libraries, while an object file depends on source code and headers.

An example of calling Make from the command line to execute a "release" target would be as follows:

```
>make -f atm.mak release
```

Here the "-f" option is used to specify the name of the makefile to be used (atm.mak) and the target to be executed is the "release" target.

One of the most important things to note is that Make in itself is not a compiler, rather it invokes your compiler either using the rules that you specify or using its own built-in rules.

---

[2] Another name for a dependency is a "prerequisite".

An Example

An example of a GNU makefile to compile a set of C++ classes (for an ATM application) and produce a releasable ".tar" file is illustrated in Listing 1.

```
01:  CXX := g++ -c
02:  CXXFLAGS := -O2
03:  LD := g++ -o
04:  LIBS := -lstdc++
05:  RM := rm -r
06:  ARCHIVE := tar -cf
07:  COMPRESS := gzip
08:  PROGRAM := atm
09:  SOURCES := account.cc customer.cc transaction.cc ↵
         atm.cc
10:  HEADERS := account.h customer.h transaction.h
11:  OBJECTS := $(SOURCES:%.cc=%.o)
12:
13:  .PHONY: all
14:  all: $(PROGRAM)
15:
16:  # redefine compilation procedure for .cc files
17:  .SUFFIXES:
18:  .SUFFIXES: .cc .o
19:  .cc.o:
20:      $(CXX) $(CXXFLAGS) $<
21:
22:  # create the executable
23:  $(PROGRAM): $(OBJECTS)
24:      $(LD) $@ $(OBJECTS) $(LIBS)
25:
26:  # dependencies (without makedepend)
27:  $(OBJECTS): $(HEADERS)
28:
```

```
29:   # create a release
30:   .PHONY: release
31:   release:
32:       $(RM) $(PROGRAM).tar.gz
33:       $(ARCHIVE) $(PROGRAM).tar $(PROGRAM) $(SRC)↵
            $(HEADERS) Makefile
34:       $(COMPRESS) $(PROGRAM).tar
35:
36:   # create a clean environment
37:   .PHONY: clean
38:   clean:
39:       $(RM) $(PROGRAM) $(OBJECTS)
```

Listing 1 – Example GNU makefile

If this makefile was used to build the ATM application then the output result would look similar to the following:

```
>make -f atm.mak
g++ -O2 -c -o account.o account.cc
g++ -O2 -c -o customer.o customer.cc
g++ -O2 -c -o transaction.o transaction.cc
g++ -O2 -c -o atm.o atm.cc
g++ -o atm account.o customer.o transaction.o atm.o ↵
    -lstdc++


>make -f atm.mak release
rm -f atm.tar.gz
tar -cf atm.tar atm account.h transaction.h ... Makefile
gzip atm.tar
```

In this makefile an executable called atm is being built, it consists of four C++ source files (as listed on line 9) and three headers file (as listed on line 10). Lines 1-11 define some Make **macros** to be used throughout the makefile. A macro in Make is a variable, it can either be user defined (as for example PROGRAM in this example) or internally pre-defined (such as $@). There are a large number of pre-defined macros[3]. Of particular note is line 11 which uses macro string substitution to create the macro OBJECTS which is similar to SOURCES but with the ".cc" extension replaced with ".o". Line 14 defines the default "all" target of the makefile - which will build the application and then create a release from it. The "all" target is marked as a ".PHONY" target (on line 13) to indicate that it is a special internal only target - otherwise make would try to check for the existence of this target on the file system.

Lines 17 to 20 define how to create object files from C++ source files via use of **suffix rules**. In practice there is no need to define such rules as Make has a large number of internal rules for most source files types. However in this case it is included to illustrate how C++ object files are constructed (and to help you with your understanding). The "$<" string is one of Make's special dynamic macros that can be used to refer to the name of the dependency file (i.e. the C++ source file being compiled). Note that one of the most annoying issues with Make is that it insists all indentation is carried out using tabs not spaces - this is true for the command script of every target.

In lines 23-24 a target is defined to link the application and lists the object files that it is dependent upon. The command on line 24 defines how to link the object files together to produce the resultant application executable. As well as listing the dependencies for object files, on line 27 we also list the dependencies of the object files on the header files which are used in their compilation. The reason for this is that if a header file is updated we want make to see that the date and time-stamp of the header file has changed and therefore automatically work out which object files it needs to rebuild.

---

[3] which can be listed by running "make -p".

Lines 31-34 define a target to create a releasable ".tar" file (including all sources and the compiled application). Finally lines 37-39 define a target that can be called to "clean up" (i.e. remove) any pre-built objects and application files in order to be able to return to a known state.

Managing Dependencies

Manually managing the header file dependencies for an application such as this is relatively straightforward; however in large applications (potentially consisting of thousands of files) this is not practical. Instead it is better to let Make and your compiler manage these dependencies for you. Most modern compilers take a command line argument to indicate that source files should be parsed for dependency information and the results output. For the GNU C/C++ compilers this is the "-M" for full or "MM" for project specific dependencies (i.e. only the header files that you have developed - not operating system header files). A simple method of managing dependencies is to add a target to create a specific dependency file and then include the output of this file directly within your makefile. An example of achieving this is illustrated in Listing 2.

```
01:  CXX := g++
02:  CXXFLAGS := -O2
03:  LD := g++ -o
04:  LIBS := -lstdc++
05:  RM := rm -f
06:  ARCHIVE := tar -cf
07:  COMPRESS := gzip
08:  PROGRAM := atm.exe
09:  SOURCES := ${wildcard *.cc}
10:  OBJECTS := $(SOURCES:%.cc=%.o)
11:
12:  .PHONY: all
```

```
13:   all: $(PROGRAM)
14:
15:   -include depend
16:
17:   # create the executable
18:   $(PROGRAM): depend $(OBJECTS)
19:       $(LD) $@ $(OBJECTS) $(LIBS)
20:
21:   # create the dependency file
22:   depend: $(SOURCES)
23:       $(CXX) -MM $(CXXFLAGS) $^ > $@
24:
25:   # create the release
26:   .PHONY: release
27:   release: $(PROGRAM)
28:       $(RM) $(PROGRAM).tar.gz
29:       $(ARCHIVE) $(PROGRAM).tar $(PROGRAM) $(SRC)↵
                $(SOURCES) ${wildcard *.h} Makefile
30:       $(COMPRESS) $(PROGRAM).tar
31:
32:   # create a clean environment
33:   .PHONY: clean
34:   clean:
35:       $(RM) $(PROGRAM).tar.gz $(PROGRAM) $(OBJECTS)
36:
37:   # clean up dependency file
38:   .PHONY: clean-depend
39:   clean-depend: clean
40:       $(RM) depend
```

Listing 2 – GNU makefile with managed dependencies

In this example a new target called "depend" is added on lines 21-23 which takes the name of each source file (via the "$^" dynamic macro) and creates a file called `depend`. Notice that on line 15 a "-include" command is used to include this file into the makefile (the minus sign means ignore errors - in case the file does not exist yet). There is also an additional cleanup target called "clean-depend" on lines 38-40. The reason that there is a special target for this is so that Make can be used to manage this dependency file, i.e. update it when it is out of date, and not for it to be deleted as part of a build specific "clean" process

If this makefile was now used to build the ATM application then the output result would look similar to the following:

```
>make -f atm.mak depend
g++ -MM -O2 account.cc atm.cc customer.cc transaction.cc↵
   > depend


>make -f atm.mak
g++ -O2 -c -o account.o account.cc
g++ -O2 -c -o customer.o customer.cc
g++ -O2 -c -o transaction.o transaction.cc
g++ -O2 -c -o atm.o atm.cc
g++ -o atm account.o customer.o transaction.o atm.o ↵
   -lstdc++


>cat depend
account.o: account.cc account.h
atm.o: atm.cc account.h customer.h transaction.h
customer.o: customer.cc customer.h account.h
transaction.o: transaction.cc transaction.h
```

The last command line invocation is used to show the contents of the dependency file.

Note, that in a large code base you might also use one of GNU Make's functions to work out the list of source files to build for you by looking in a specific directory. A typical example is shown on line 9 where the GNU make "${wildcard *.cc}" function is being used to select all of the source files with the extension ".cc".

Issues with Make

There are a number of potential issues with Make which can be summarized as follows:

- **Maintaining dependencies** – As already discussed this is not a trivially exercise with Make. If you implement Make recursively then it is also possible to generate incomplete or circular dependencies.

- **Portability** – Since Make uses operating system specific commands to carry out its actions, writing portable makefiles can be difficult.

- **Clock skew** – The use of modification time stamps to determine when a file has been updated can be error prone over distributed file systems such as NFS.

- **Obscure syntax** - Make has a very strict requirement for indentation - only tabs and no other white space characters can be used. The use of obscure symbols for targets and dependencies means makefiles are not the easiest of assets to maintain.

- **Debugging** – There is no natural debugger for makefiles, so working out why make did or did not do something can be difficult and time consuming.

- **Speed** – In isolation Make build processes can be quite slow – especially implementations of recursive Make which recurse up and down complex directory structure. Typically distributed compilation is used to reduce total build times.

Writing and maintaining makefiles is an acquired skill. Since its is easy to write makefiles that are unreadable by less skilled individuals, most projects require one or more dedicated Build Engineers or use a central Build Team.

Alternatives to Make

There are a number of alternatives to using Make on C and C++ projects. Popular open-source or free alternatives include **Jam** (www.perforce.com/jam/jam.html) which understands C and C++ dependencies, and **SCons** (www.scons.org) a cross language software construction tool whose scripts are written in the popular Python (www.python.org) programming language. Commercial alternatives include the mature IBM Rational ClearCase **clearmake**[4] tool and the powerful **ElectricAccelerator**[5] tool from Electric Cloud. Both of these tools automatically manage dependency information and offer sophisticated build distribution and build avoidance capabilities.

Java

Like C and C++, Java source code is also compiled, but not to directly executable code. Instead it is first compiled to bytecode – assembly language like instructions – which in turn is then executed by a Java Virtual Machine (JVM). This capability allows an application to be executed without re-compilation on any operating system platform for which a JVM has been implemented. JVM technology is one of the main reasons for the success of Java. One of the downsides to this

---

[4] www-306.ibm.com/software/awdtools/clearcase/
[5] www.electric-cloud.com/products/electricaccelerator.php

though, is that Java applications will inevitably execute more slowly than equivalent C or C++ ones.

Although not strictly an open source application itself, Java has a very open development eco-system. There are a multitude of reusable component libraries, development frameworks and application server platforms that can be used to help shorten the overall Java development lifecycle. This can mean that there is significantly less code required to develop a Java application than there would to develop an equivalent C or C++ one. It also means that builds have less to compile and can execute much faster (in most projects significantly less than an hour).

Using pre-built components, frameworks and server platforms might make the overall Java compilation process quicker and simpler, but it also results in two additional tasks that have to be carried out and which can significantly affect the overall build process:

- managing the composite set of libraries and their dependencies,
- coordinating and controlling deployment of an application to multiple server platforms.

Open source libraries are very common in Java, so common that if you make use of a number of application frameworks and components you might find that you have multiple versions of the same library. Managing the composite set of libraries that your applications make use of has always been a source of frustration for Java developers and Buildmeisters.

The second issue here really only affects Java applications which need to be installed into some form of run-time container, e.g., a Web application into Apache Tomcat or a J2EE application into IBM WebSphere Application Server. Such applications are typically deployed to many environments, e.g., Integration, System Test, User Acceptance Test and Production, and the application might be required to be "configured" differently for each one. This configuration will often be carried out as part of the build process. Therefore, although a Java application might have a relatively short compile time, it can unfortunately have a long total build and deploy time. I will look in more detail at the issues of deploying an application to multiple environments in chapters 6 and 7.

The build scripting technology that is typically used for Java applications is Apache Ant (http://ant.apache.org).

Overview of Apache Ant

Apache Ant is currently the most common Java build scripting tool. Created by James Duncan Davidson while working on an open source project (which later became Apache Tomcat[6]); Ant was developed as a platform neutral build scripting tool for Java projects. Apache Ant was officially released as a standalone product in 2000 and is now the most widely used Java build scripting tool.

In its simplest form, Ant can be used to create and coordinate a sequence of individual build commands. One of the main benefits of Ant, is that like Java itself, Ant is platform neutral and therefore an Ant build script can be executed on any supported Java platform. Ant implements a simple form of build avoidance, in that it looks at the date and time stamps of individual files to work out what (if any) of the files from your complete application it needs to re-build.

The input to Ant is a textual build script by default called `build.xml` (although any filename can be used). A complete application can be built using one or many build scripts (which are commonly located at different component or directory levels). Each build script describes a set of **targets**, which are the core parts of the

---

[6] http://tomcat.apache.org/

composite build process, e.g. compile source code, unit test, create a Java archive and so on.

Each of the targets can make reference to any of Ant's built-in **tasks**. A task is basically an interface to a Java object written to carry out a predefined operation, e.g. compile a set of source files, delete a directory structure and so on. Parameters can be specified for the task, defining its exact invocation. There are a large number of built-in tasks (see the Ant manual for details[7]), however since the tasks are interfaces to Java objects, you can quite easily extend Ant by creating new tasks yourselves.

An example of calling Ant from the command line to execute a "release" target would be as follows:

```
>ant -f atm.xml release
```

Here the "-f" option is used to specify the name of the build script that you wish to use (atm.xml) and the target which will be executed is the "release" target.

One of the most important things to note is that Ant in itself is not a compiler, rather it invokes your Java compiler "javac" through its built-in <javac> task. This task, recursively scans source and destination directories to look for Java classes that need to be (re)built and optimizes calls to the Java compiler.

An Example

An example of an Ant build script to compile a set of Java classes (for an ATM application) and produce a releasable ".jar" file is illustrated in Listing 3.

---

[7] http://ant.apache.org/manual/index.html

```
01:   <?xml version="1.0">
02:
03:   <project name="atm" default="compile" basedir=".">
04:     <property name="dir.src"   value="src"/>
05:     <property name="dir.build" value="build"/>
06:     <property name="dir.dist"  value="dist"/>
07:     <property name="dir.libs" ↵
                value="C:\JavaTools\libs"/>
08:
09:     <!-- classpath used throughout the project -->
10:     <path id="classpath">
11:         <pathelement location="${dir.build}/>
12:         <!-- include third party libraries -->
13:         <fileset dir="${dir.libs}">
14:             <include name="*.jar"/>
15:         </fileset>
16:     </path>
17:
18:   <!-- initialise directory structure -->
19:   <target name="init" description="initialise ↵
        directory structure">
20:     <mkdir dir="${dir.build}"/>
21:     <mkdir dir="${dir.dist}"/>
22:   </target>
23:
24:   <!-- remove generated files -->
25:   <target name="clean" description="remove ↵
        generated files">
26:     <delete dir="${dir.build}"/>
27:     <delete dir="${dir.dist}"/>
28:   </target>
29:
30:   <!-- compile source code -->
31:   <target name="compile" depends="init" ↵
```

```
            description="compile source code">
32:     <javac destdir="${dir.build}" >
33:         <src path="${dir.src}"/>
34:         <classpath refid="classpath"/>
35:     </javac>
37:   </target>
38:
39:   <!-- create distribution archive -->
40:   <target name="dist" depends="compile" ↵
          description="create distribution archive">
41:     <jar jarfile="${dir.dist}/${ant.project.name}.jar"
42:         basedir="${dir.build}"
43:         includes="**/*.class">
44:   </target>
45:
46: </project>
```

Listing 3 – Example Ant build file

If this build script was used to build the ATM application then the output result would look similar to the following:

```
>ant -f atm.xml clean
Buildfile: atm.xml

clean:

BUILD SUCCESSFUL
Total time: 1 seconds

>ant -f atm.xml
Buildfile atm.xml

init:
```

```
[mkdir] Created dir:C:\Build\ATM\build
[mkdir] Created dir:C:\Build\ATM\dist

compile:
    [javac] Compiling 4 source files to C:\Build\ATM\build

BUILD SUCCESSFUL
Total Time: 4 seconds
```

In this build script a Java archive called `atm.jar` is being built. There are four targets: `init`, `clean`, `compile` and `dist`. Sometimes a target will have a dependency on another target, for example before you create a distribution ("`.jar`") file, you would need to compile the source code. These dependencies are easily specified via a `depends` attribute in the target. You can see this with the dist target on line 40 (where the target requires the "`compile`" target to be executed first). Ant will automatically execute any dependencies.

You will see that on lines 4-7 the script makes reference to property values. In Ant, **properties** are equivalent to most programming language's concept of variable constants; that is to say they are immutable and once properties have been assigned a value they cannot be changed. Here they are being used to define directory names. You make references to properties by using the `${property_name}` symbols (see line 11 for an example). An interesting feature of properties is that they can be overridden from the command line. For example, if you wanted to override the `dir.build` property, you could use the following:

```
>ant -f atm.xml compile -Ddir.build=bin
```

If you are compiling source code in Java you will need to define a **Classpath**. This is the combination of libraries containing pre-built classes that you need to build against. In lines 10-16 a classpath is defined which looks at the build directory as well as a set of third party ".jar" files held at the location C:\JavaTools\lib.

One final point worthy of note is the use of Ant's built in variables. In this example, on line 41 I am using the ${ant.project.name} variable when creating a ".jar" file, this refers to the project name "atm" as defined on line 3, so the name of the ".jar" file will be atm.jar.

Issues with Apache Ant

There are a number of potential issues with Ant which can be summarized as follows:

- **Maintaining library dependencies** – As already discussed, maintaining the list of version dependencies for projects using a large amount of open-source components can be time consuming and potentially error prone.[8]

- **Portability** – Although Ant build scripts are inherently portable, you still need to account for operating system path variants (e.g. "C:\" on Windows versus "/" on UNIX) and embed the logic in your script accordingly[9].

- **Debugging** – Like Make there is no natural debugger for Ant, so working out why Ant did or did not do something can be difficult and time consuming.

- **XML Syntax** – XML is not a natural language for

---

[8] Two solutions to managing library dependencies with Ant are Apache Ivy (http://ant.apache.org/ivy/) or the Ant tasks for Apache Maven (http://maven.apache.org/ant-tasks.html).
[9] See [LeeABM07] for details on how to achieve this.

humans to read and was not designed to be concise. Therefore it is relatively easy to end up with large build scripts.

- **Properties** – As already discussed properties in Ant are immutable! They are not variables as per your usual programming language. Also you cannot use one property to hold the "name" of another property and resolve it at reference time.

In my opinion it is relatively easy to get Apache Ant working for small to medium sized projects, however for large projects with potentially multiple build scripts it can become unwieldy quite quickly. If the build scripts are well maintained and a number of best practices are followed then it is still possible to manage large projects with Ant. There are a number of good books to help you achieve this including *Ant in Action* [Loughran07] and *Apache Ant – The Buildmeister's Guide* [LEEABM07].

Alternatives to Apache Ant

In order to improve script maintenance issues and to help with library dependency management, Apache Maven (http://maven.apache.org) was introduced as an alternative Java build scripting tool. Apache Maven also uses XML as its input format; however it provides more of a "framework" for the build process and therefore the amount of scripting that is required – even for large projects – can be significantly less than Apache Ant.

Microsoft .NET

All of Microsoft's .NET development languages such as C#.NET or Visual Basic.NET are compiled to Microsoft's equivalent of bytecode - **managed code**. As a result, earlier languages such as Microsoft C and Visual Basic are now said to produce unmanaged code. Since managed code technology is equivalent to the Java JVM technology, the same types of issues that affect the Java build process also affect the Microsoft .NET build process. One of the main differences however, is that since the Microsoft development environment is not as "open" as Java[10], Microsoft obviously has more control over the development environment, its build tools and integrations.

In the early versions of Microsoft Visual Studio, a variant of Make was supplied as the preferred build scripting tool. Although this has been used in many projects, it has not proved very popular due to the obscurity of Make and the limited integration of Microsoft's variant into the Visual Studio development environment. Consequently, with the introduction of the .NET framework Microsoft took the opportunity to introduce a new build scripting tool called MSBuild (http://blogs.msdn.com/msbuild) that was more integrated and aware of the overall development environment.

Overview of MSBuild

MSBuild is based on similar concepts to Ant; build scripts are written in XML and they have an understanding of the .NET domain. The input to MSBuild is a textual build script usually with a ".proj" extension (although it can effectively be any name). The Visual Studio.NET development environment automatically generates MSBuild build scripts for any of your projects, for example, for a C# project named "ATM" an ATM.csproj build script would be produced. This build script would be created, updated and used directly from inside the IDE. In practice you can either update the project build scripts directly, or as is more common, write additional

---

[10] Although the Mono open source project (www.mono-project.com) does provide the necessary software to develop and run .NET client and server applications on many different platforms.

MSBuild script that act as wrappers around them, calling a number of Visual Studio.NET projects and executing additional operations.

Each build scripts describes a set of **targets**, which are the core parts of the composite build process, e.g. compile source code, unit test, create a .NET assembly and so on. Each of the targets can make reference to any of MSBuild's pre-defined **tasks** – which are supplied with the development environment. There are a large number of tasks (see the MSBuild task reference for details[11]), however since the tasks are interfaces to .NET objects, you can quite easily extend MSBuild by creating new tasks yourselves.

An example of calling MSBuild from the command line to execute a "Release" target would be as follows:

```
>msbuild atmbuild.proj /t:Release
```

Here the "-/t:" option is used to specify the target which will be executed.

An Example

An example of an MSBuild build script to compile a set of C# classes (for an ATM application), and archive the results into a Zip file is illustrated in Listing 4.

```
01:   <?xml version="1.0" encoding="utf-8" ?>
02:   <Project xmlns="http://schemas.microsoft.com/
         developer/msbuild/2003" DefaultTargets="Dist">
03:
04:     <!-- include MSBuild Community tasks →
05:     <Import Project="$(MSBuildExtensionsPath)\ ↩
```

---

[11] http://msdn2.microsoft.com/en-us/library/7z253716.aspx

```
         MSBuildCommunityTasks\MSBuild.Community.Tasks.
         Targets"/>
06:
07:    <!-- project properties -->
08:    <PropertyGroup>
09:      <Configuration Condition=" '$(Configuration)' ↵
           == '' ">Debug</Configuration>
10:      <OutputDirectory>Dist</OutputDirectory>
11:      <AppVersion>1.0</AppVersion>
12:      <ZipFilename>$(MSBuildProjectName)- ↵
           $(Configuration)-$(AppVersion).zip</ZipFilename>
13:    </PropertyGroup>
14:
15:    <!-- Debug properties -->
16:    <PropertyGroup Condition=" '$(Configuration)' ↵
           == 'Debug' ">
17:      <OutputPath>bin\Debug\</OutputPath>
18:    </PropertyGroup>

19:    <!-- Release properties -->
20:    <PropertyGroup Condition=" '$(Configuration)' ↵
           == 'Release' ">
21:      <OutputPath>bin\Release\</OutputPath>
22:    </PropertyGroup>
23:
24:    <!-- project Items -->
25:    <ItemGroup>
26:      <ZipFiles Include="$(OutputPath)\*.exe"/>
27:      <ZipFiles Include="$(OutputPath)\*.dll"/>
28:      <ZipFiles Include="$(OutputPath)\**\*.dat"/>
29:      <ProjectReferences Include="*.*csproj" />
30:    </ItemGroup>
31:
32:    <!-- initialize directory structure -->
33:    <Target Name="Init">
```

```
34:      <MakeDir Directories="$(OutputDirectory)"
35:        Condition="!Exists('$(OutputDirectory)')"/>
36:    </Target>
37:
38:    <!-- remove generated files -->
39:    <Target Name="Clean">
40:      <MSBuild Projects="@(ProjectReferences)"
41:        Targets="Clean" />
42:      <RemoveDir Directories="$(OutputDirectory)"
43:        Condition="Exists('$(OutputDirectory)')" />
44:      <Delete Files="$(ZipFilename)" />
45:    </Target>
46:
47:    <!-- compile source code -->
48:    <Target Name="Compile" DependsOnTargets="Init">
49:      <MSBuild Projects="@(ProjectReferences)" />
50:    </Target>
51:
52:    <!-- create distribution archive -->
53:    <Target Name="Dist" DependsOnTargets="Compile">
54:      <Zip Files="@(ZipFiles)"
55:        ZipFileName="$(ZipFilename)"
56:        WorkingDirectory="$(OutputDirectory)" />
57:    </Target>
58:
59: </Project>
```

Listing 4 – Example MSBuild build script

In this build script there are four targets: Init, Clean, Compile and Dist. Sometimes a target will have a dependency on another target, for example before you create a distribution (".zip") file, you would need to compile the source code. These dependencies are easily specified via a DependsOnTargets attribute in the target. You can see this with the `Dist` target on line 53 (where the target requires the `Compile` target to be executed first). MSBuild will automatically execute any dependencies.

You will see that on lines 7-13 the script creates a **PropertyGroup** that contains **properties** to be used throughout the project. Although properties are defined and referenced differently in MSBuild to Ant, they essentially fulfil the same purpose as key/value pairs. Here the properties are being used to define the output directories and name of the Zip file. You make references to properties by using the `$(property_name)` symbols (see line 12 for an example). Individual properties and PropertyGroup's can also have conditions; this allows properties to be set dependent on the value of other properties. For example, on lines 20-22 a PropertyGroup is defined where the value of the `OutputPath` property will be set to "`bin\Release\`" only if the property `Configuration` has previously been set to "`Release`". You would typically use this capability by overriding the value of the `Configuration` property from the command line as follows:

```
>msbuild atmbuild.proj /p:Configuration=Release
```

In order to specify collections of resources (such as files) and metadata, MSBuild has the concept of **Items** and **ItemGroups**. An Item defines an input to the build process and are typically used as parameters for tasks. For example on lines 26-28 a `ZipFiles` item collection is defined to specify all of the files that are to be included in the distribution archive. You can make reference to items by using the `@(item_name)` symbols (see line 54 for an example). Like properties and PropertyGroups, items can also have conditions.

If this build script was used to build the ATM application then the output result would look similar to the following:

```
>msbuild atmbuild.proj /t:Clean
Build started 27/10/2007 18:15:26.
```

```
Project "C:\...\ATM\ATMBuild.proj" (Clean target(s)):

Target Clean:

    Project "C:\...\ATM\ATMBuild.proj" is building
    "C:\...\ATM\ATM.csproj" (Clean target(s)):

Build succeeded.
    0 Warning(s)
    0 Error(s)

Time Elapsed 00:00:00.07
```

>ant atmbuild.proj /t:Dist

```
Build started 27/10/2007 18:17:15.

Project "C:\...\ATM\ATM\ATMBuild.proj" (Dist target(s)):
Target Init:
    Creating directory "Dist".
Target Compile:

    Project "C:\...\ATM\ATMBuild.proj" is building
    "C:\...\ATM\ATM.csproj" (default targets):

    Target CoreCompile:
    C:\WINDOWS\Microsoft.NET\Framework\v2.0.50727\Csc.exe
    ... /out:obj\Debug\ATM.exe ...
    Done building project "ATM.csproj".
Target Dist:
    Creating zip file "ATMBuild-Debug-1.0.zip".
      added "bin/Debug/ATM.exe".
      added "bin/Debug/ATM.dll".

      ...
    Created zip file "ATMBuild-Debug-1.0.zip"
    successfully.
```

```
Build succeeded.
    0 Warning(s)
    0 Error(s)

Time Elapsed 00:00:00.45
```

Note that the Zip task is not part of the standard MSBuild tasks but is available from the MSBuild community tasks project web site (http://msbuildtasks.tigris.org/)

Issues with MSBuild

There are a number of potential issues with MSBuild which can be summarized as follows:

- **Documentation** – MSBuild is still relatively new and there is not the same amount of either hardcopy or electronic information that is available with either Make or Apache Ant.

- **Visual Studio.NET Integration** – Although MSBuild scripts can be edited from within the Visual Studio.NET environment, the integration is not as comprehensive as you would expect for a Microsoft engineered environment. For example there are no templates or wizards and in the current version you have to add MSBuild as an external tool.

- **Release Packaging** – Currently there is limited task support for creating release packages (setup.exe or Microsoft Installer ".msi" files) using MSBuild from the command line. Current strategies include using additional toolkilts such as Windows Installer XML (Wix) (http://wix.sourceforge.net/).

- **Debugging** – Like Make and Ant there is no natural debugger for MSBuild, so working out why it did or did not do something can be difficult and time consuming.

- **XML Syntax** – As with Ant, XML is not a natural language for humans to read and was not designed to be concise. Therefore it is relatively easy to end up with large build scripts.

In my opinion MSBuild is a well designed and powerful build scripting tool. Its designers have learnt lessons from the implementation of earlier tools such as Make and Ant and made MSBuild powerful but still relatively simple to use. Although it is still relatively new, the fact that MSBuild files can be generated and edited from within the Visual Studio IDE and its tasks extended using .NET objects make it just about my favourite build scripting tool.

Alternatives to MSBuild

There is also an open source equivalent of Apache Ant for building .NET projects called NAnt (http://nant.sourceforge.net/); however with the advent of the Microsoft supported MSBuild technology, over time I believe that NAnt will probably only retain limited popularity.

Interpreted Languages

There are a large amount of scripting or interpreted languages, such as Perl (www.perl.org), Python (www.python.org) and Ruby (www.ruby-lang.org). These languages have no direct compilation process; instead they are usually run straight through an interpreter (or an internalised equivalent of bytecode). This obviously means that they will execute slower than compiled (or compiled to bytecode) languages such as C and C++, Java or VS.NET. However with the performance of modern operating systems and hardware this is becoming less critical.

The overall time to develop and deliver is significantly less with interpreted languages; they are therefore potentially interesting solutions for time-to-market critical applications. Ruby in particular has been used as an alternative to Java on a number of projects. Without a direct compilation process, there is sometimes a belief that no build process is required; however all of the build functions that are required for integration in a team environment such as Static Analysis, Unit Testing and Code Coverage still apply.

Most interpreted languages have their own build scripting tools, for example **SCons** (www.scons.org) for Python and **Rake** (http://rake.rubyforge.org) for Ruby. Note that interpreted languages can also form an important part of an overall build process, especially where complex command scripting is required.

Summary

Selecting, learning and implementing build scripts using a language specific build scripting tool will take a large amount of your time and effort. Across an organization, it is common to have many projects, implemented in different languages and each using their own build scripting tool. As a corporate Buildmeister you might therefore have to understand multiple technologies and tools – not an easy task. Hopefully however, this chapter has given you a flavour of the different types of tools that are out there and how they work.

In the next chapter, I will look move away from looking at technology to discuss how the choice of different development methods can affect the build process.

CHAPTER 4

Build Process Environments:

Development Methods

It is common sense to take a method and try it. If it fails, admit it
frankly and try another. But above all, try something.
Franklin D. Roosevelt

In addition to being affected by specific development languages, any
build process will also be affected by a project's chosen development
method. Similarly, it can also be affected by the vertical industry that
the organization is operating in. In this chapter, I will look at a
number of popular development methods and describe what
requirements of the build process they make.

Development methods

If there is one thing that is guaranteed to be the cause of emotional
debate and discussion in the software development community it is the
choice of development method or process. In this section my intention
is not to enter into this debate and discuss which method is best, rather
it is establish what requirements of the build process different

development methods make. Although there is some commonality, I believe there are subtle differences in the implementation of a build process to support different development methods and which I will aim to bring to light.

Agile Development

Agile development encompasses a number of distinct methods such as eXtreme Programming (XP), Dynamic Systems Development Method (DSDM), and Scrum. All of the methods are related in that they subscribe to the basic premises of the Agile manifesto [AgileM01], co-written by several luminaries of the software development world. The fundamental principle of the Agile manifesto is recognising the value of:

- Individuals and interactions over processes and tools
- Working software over comprehensive documentation
- Customer collaboration over contract negotiation
- Responding to change over following a plan

Although Agile methods were introduced as new and somewhat controversial mechanisms for delivering software development projects, today Agile development practices such as Incremental Development, Test Driven Development, and Continuous Integration are commonplace and have been accepted and absorbed as an alternative approach to software development.

The approach that most Agile methods share is the direct involvement and interaction with users or customers, and the development of functionality in frequent, short iterations (usually between two to twelve weeks). Typically, at the start of each iteration, Agile teams negotiate with the customer to define new features or change requests. These are estimated by the developers and then subsequently prioritized by the customer for the next iteration, as illustrated in Figure 9.

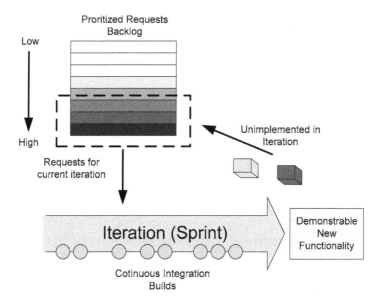

Figure 9 - Example Agile method

A **backlog** of any features or change requests that have not been implemented in an iteration are kept and, together with any new requests, are re-prioritized by the customer for the next iteration. Developers are permitted to work on requests for the current iteration or to carry out re-factoring and simplification of existing code as necessary. The intention behind this is to keep design simple and prevent gratuitous feature bloat. Code is also Continuously Integrated; which means it is implemented, tested, and committed frequently in very small units, with an automated build process being invoked at commit time to check for integration errors.

Feature Drops

Although Agile methods generally proscribe continual testing at the development level; for internal, more system oriented testing Feature Drops are often made available. These are not intended to be end of iteration, customer consumable builds. Instead they are development builds but with specific completed and testable features. Feature Drops allow career Testers to exercise a product and customer representatives to visualize its content and steer it in the right direction.

I am a great believer in Agile software development practices, in particular the following four practices:

- **Incremental development** – developing system features in small, frequent iterations and implementing high risk items first.

- **Refactoring** – restructuring a system without changing its behaviour to remove duplication, simplify or add flexibility.

- **Continuous testing**. – driving system development through the creation of unit and customer tests.

- **Continuous integration** – integrating and building the entire system (potentially) many times a day to reduce integration time and errors.

I have implemented and observed these practices many times where they have ultimately proven successful in helping projects to deliver quality software in a timely manner. In essence though, these practices are simply part of a common-sense **risk driven development** approach. Consequently, their implementation has evolved beyond their initial Agile development roots and are now part of many enterprise and organizational software development processes which probably would not consider themselves fully "Agile"[1].

If you are implementing Agile development methods, then I would expect the following requirements to be made of the build process:

- **Automated Continuous Integration Builds** – builds are usually triggered on an event such as atomic commit by a developer to the code repository.

- **Accessible Build Scripts** – Agile methods promote collective code ownership, which means any developer can change a file. Consequently, every user should be able to execute the build or have it executed for them.

- **Comprehensive Static Analysis and Unit Testing functions** – to ensure that developers can successfully integrate their changes as part of an ongoing development effort.

- **Short build times** – typically of less than 10 minutes.

- **A dedicated Build Server** - upon which the Continuous Integration builds are carried out.

Agile development with its incremental development and frequent integration paradigm obviously places a strong emphasis on a consistent, automated and repeatable build process. Most Agile teams I have worked with have had a very good "technical" build process. However, one area where I have often seen such teams lacking is in defining a consistent approach to deployment. This is especially true

---

[1] The Unified Process (http://en.wikipedia.org/wiki/Unified_Process) for example has had many of these practices embedded in its core for years.

where different user groups are involved in deploying an application to its run-time environments.

Feature Driven Development

Not every Agile development method necessarily shares the same requirements of the build process. One example that is worth mentioning is Feature Driven Development (FDD). FDD is generally accepted as an Agile method in that it promotes incremental change by small teams, however it also promotes more upfront design and class (or component) ownership rather than collective code ownership.

In FDD, a Feature Team is constructed that consists of a small team of developers (say 4 or 5) who are experts on the particular classes that will be required to be changed in order to implement a specific new feature. Developers might potentially be part of more than one Feature Team, but for each feature a chief programmer (or Feature Lead) is assigned. When the feature has been completed it is typically up to the chief programmer to integrate it into the project's overall Integration Build.

As a result, internal to the Feature Team they might adopt build processes akin to those described for Agile development. However they might also mix in some of the build requirements of traditional Enterprise development methods (which will be discussed next). For example, since Feature teams will potentially need to work in parallel and in isolation, they might adopt Staged Integration and adopt a Continuous Integration build for their team.

Traditional Enterprise development

Traditional Enterprise development encompasses methods such as the Rational Unified Process (RUP) or Team Software Process (TSP) which have been adopted by many large software development projects, usually in large corporate or commercial environments. This has included projects (or programmes of work) to implement such systems as: missile defence systems, telecommunications switches, government taxation systems or financial services trading platforms. These types of projects might take many years to implement, and are done so by different teams, potentially from different companies or organizations.

Traditional Enterprise methods tend to me more plan-driven with more focus on design and architecture - because of the size and nature of the applications that are being developed. The implementation approach most Enterprise development projects take is to develop as components - either common (team based services) or functional (through logical decomposition). Each component typically has its own development team and at regular milestones (say once a week) component code is delivered and integrated into a System Integration Build – at which point a new System Baseline is created. This process is illustrated in Figure 10.

If you are implementing Enterprise development, then I would expect the following requirements to be made of the build process:

- **Dedicated Build Engineers** – who are responsible for creating and executing what can be quite complex build processes. They act as a central function ensuring build practices are implemented across discrete component teams.

- **Reuseable and Secure Build Scripts** – With multiple component projects, it is typical to define build scripts per component. Common build routines should be shared and reused to reduce time and effort as well as to promote best practices. When build routines are shared they should be securely managed as any uncontrolled or erroneous changes can potentially affect all of the component teams.

- **Automated Daily Builds** – to ensure that components can be successfully integrated as part of an ongoing development effort.

- **Comprehensive Component Integration and Functional Integration Testing functions** – to ensure the quality and functionality of integrated components.

- **A shared Build Server Infrastructure** - upon which the Component Integration and System Integration Builds are carried out.

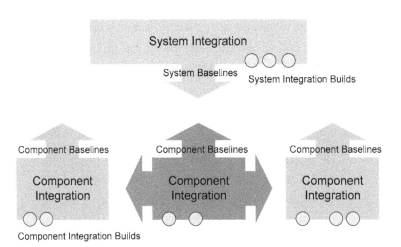

Figure 10 - Example Enterprise Development Method

Note that not every software development project that is carried out in an "Enterprise" organization will be the same. For example, Financial Services companies usually have significant amounts of developers (maybe several thousand) but most would be working on relatively small development projects. In this case, the requirements for the build process would generally follow more closely that of Agile development - with potentially an additional automated reporting capability to satisfy organizational compliance concerns.

Open source development

Open source development is a well known method of developing "free-to-use, free-to-modify" software applications. Open source projects provide complete visibility of the source code base and their development plans. They are typically implemented by a community of "volunteers". These are either developers who decide to use their free time to work on the project (because they have a direct interest), or they are developers from organizations who have a vested interest in the outcome of the project. Whatever the reasons, there are typically three generic roles that are inherent in open source projects and which can be summarised as follows:

- **Users** – direct customers or users of the developed application, and who are typically not involved in its development.
- **Contributors** – users of the application who find a bug or require a new feature in the application. In "closed" development projects, they would normally have to wait for the owners of the application to address these issues, however because they have access to the source code, they can develop a fix or feature themselves and then contribute it back to the open source project for subsequent inclusion.

- **Committers** – developers who have permission to commit changes back into the code base and who develop the majority of the project's core features. Committers sanitise and incorporate contributions from Contributors into the project.

Open source projects tend to produce milestone (or stable builds) - which are released and used by the majority of Users - and development builds – which are carried out on a daily basis and used by Contributors to develop their changes. If you are implementing open source development, then I would expect the following requirements to be made of the build process:

- **Automated Daily Builds** – where the latest committed changes are built, tested and packaged up to be used by Contributors for further development.

- **Comprehensive Static Analysis and Unit Testing functions** – to ensure that any contributions are of sufficient project quality and standard.

- **Accessible Build Scripts** – open source development actively promotes user contribution. Consequently, every user should be able to execute the build.

- **A dedicated Build Server** - upon which the Daily builds are carried out.

Open source development has managed to deliver a number of significant and well used applications, such as the Linux operating system, the Apache Web Server and the Eclipse development environment. Commercial organisations (such as IBM and Red Hat) are also starting to adopt similar "open" development practices for their commercial products, providing source code access to essential interfaces, as well as more visibility of development plans, features and bugs. The intention behind this is to leverage the "community spirit" which open source projects generate and allow users to have more of an input to the direction and success of a project.

Industry sectors

The choice of software development method is not the only factor that has an impact on the build process. Often the industry in which you are working will have the biggest natural impact. Some specific examples of this include:

- **The Financial Services industry** - which typically has more requirements to meet compliance or governance mandates. In such a scenario reports, enforcement and security are often key.

- **The Multimedia or Games industry** – which typically has large amounts of data (e.g., graphics) to process, so overall build times will be long.

- **The Software Vendor industry** (i.e., Microsoft or IBM) – who typically has to develop and build end-user products for multiple platforms (e.g., Windows, Linux, UNIX). Such builds usually have to be executed on multiple platforms in parallel to save time.

Practically every industry sector will have some form of domain specific build process requirement. Even industries that develop packaged applications, where there is effectively no code, will require some form of build process – although they might not specifically call it this. I would therefore encourage you to look at the industry in which you are working and document what requirements of the build process you make today and might potentially make in the future.

Summary

There are many different software development languages, methods and industries that make different "requests" of the build process. In this chapter I have described some of the many examples. The point is that you will inevitably have to tailor and find the right build process for your own project – you can't borrow or buy a build process off the shelf that will fit exactly.

The good news however is that you can re-use some of the many different best practices, techniques and tools that are available to help in implementing your build process. The documentation of some of these best practices is obviously one of the main motivations for writing this book.

Now that I have defined and described the build process and how different environments can influence it, next I will look at a set of core skills that anyone implementing a build process should possess.

CHAPTER 5

Build Process Core Skills

How many a man has thrown up his hands at a time when a little more effort, a little more patience would have achieved success?
Elbert Hubbard

In order to implement any build process you will need a good grounding in software development basics. You do not need to be an expert in everything – except maybe build scripting tools - but you will need certainly to possess some fundamental and core skills. In this chapter I will discuss the set of core skills that I believe every Buildmeister should possess a working knowledge of.

System administration

Whenever I have been involved in implementing a new build process, at some stage I have had to carry out basic system administration tasks. These tasks have usually revolved around the setup and maintenance of the build infrastructure, e.g., setting up new servers, configuring them, adding users and so on. Often this infrastructure needs to implemented or configured rapidly when the needs of a project require it. In some organizations, the System Administration team might be flexible enough to handle this, but in others these tasks have to be carried out by the Build Team

If you do have a dedicated Build Team, I would recommend that at least one member of your team is proficient in basic System Administration tasks for your chosen operating system. If you are a contract or consulting Buildmeister I would recommend that you get a basic and recognised System Administration qualification on your Resume. You could even learn the basics at home. With open source operating systems like Linux this is relatively easy because you can download the media and setup your own network. With other operating systems it is not as easy as you will require access to the installation media and some "real hardware" to play with.

Regular expressions

A good knowledge of Regular Expressions (sometimes known as regexps or REs) is a fundamental skill that any Buildmeister should acquire. Regular expressions are a language subset common to many programming and scripting languages. They allow you to specify a set of rules, for a particular text pattern, that you want to match in some input. During the implementation of your build process, you will use regular expressions in a number of way, some examples include:

- specifying the location and name of source code files in build scripting tools – rather than having to specify every file manually.
- replacing a placeholder string in a source code file with a specific build number at build time.
- executing version control change and history commands and formatting the output into a readable release report.

The typical form of a regular expression is one that searches for a particular text string using normal and special characters, for example the regular expression abx* will find all strings containing the letters ab followed by zero or more x's, e.g., ab, abx, abxxxx and so on. There are a large number of special characters that can be used in regular expressions; a number of them are illustrated in Table 1.

Expression	Meaning
x	Match one letter, x in this case
^	Match at beginning of line
$	Match at end of line
.	Match any character (except newline)
*	Match zero or more times
+	Match one or more times
?	Match zero or one time
[xxx]	Match a set of characters
[a-z]	Match a range of characters
[^xxx]	Match characters that do not belong to the set
a|b	Match one or other character
\d	Match any digit [0-9]
\D	Match any non-digit [^0-9]
\w	Match any word [a-zA-Z_0-9] character
\W	Match any non word character
\s	Match any whitespace character
\S	Match any non whitespace character

Table 1 – Regular Expression special characters

As an example, suppose that you wanted to create a report of all the test classes in your build directory, maybe to see if one had been implemented for every source class. If you carried out a listing of the directory and wrote its content to a file, you might expect to see something like Listing 5.

```
src/com/buildmeister/Customer.java
src/com/buildmeister/Account.java
src/com/buildmeister/TestCustomer.java
src/com/buildmeister/TestAcccount.java
...
```

Listing 5 - Example directory listing

To match only Test classes (those that start with "Test" followed by a class name and ending in ".java") you could use the regular expressions as illustrated in Figure 11.

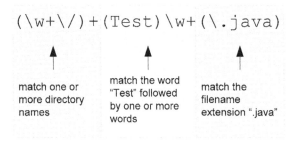

Figure 11 – Example Regular Expression

Notice the use of backslashes ("\") in Figure 11 to escape any character that would otherwise be interpreted as a special character, i.e., a period is matched by escaping it: "\.".

An example of how you could use this regular expression in a script, in this case a Perl script, is shown in Listing 6.

```
my $count = 0;
print "Test classes:\n";
while (<>) {
    if (/(\w+\/)+(Test)\w+(\.java)/) {
        print "- $_";
    }
}
print "Total = $count\n";
```

Listing 6 - Perl Script using Regular Expressions

In this example, each of the test classes is output and the total number of classes calculated. This is achieved using the following Perl scripting capabilities:

- The "while (<>)" syntax to iterate over each line of a file.

- The "if (/ ... /)" syntax to see if the regular expression is matched on a particular line. If it does then the name of the file is printed.

- And the special "$_" symbol which is Perl's way of holding the content of the current line, i.e. the name of the file.

If you executed this script with the directory listing from Listing 5 as input, then you would see output similar to Listing 7.

As you can see, regular expressions are very powerful but can be quite cryptic and initially confusing to read. Practically every language supports regular expressions in some way. Although some may have slightly different syntax the general constructs are the same. For more information on regular expressions I recommend reading *Mastering*

Regular Expressions [Friedl06] or *Regular Expression Pocket Reference* [Stubblevine03] – the later is a nice handy reference book.

```
Test classes:
- src/com/buildmeister/TestCustomer.java
- src/com/buildmeister/TestAccount.java
Total = 2
```

Listing 7 - Example output from Perl script

XML

XML (eXtensible Markup Language) is a mark-up language that was created to be able to manage, display, and organize data in a consistent and tool independent way. XML is both an input and output format. Many build scripting tools, such as Apache Ant and Microsoft MSBuild use XML as their input format. Other tools such as unit testing and code coverage tools allow their output to be written as XML. XML can be used as an independent communication mechanism between different tools and it can also be formatted as HTML for custom presentation.

At a high level, XML documents consist of elements, attributes and their relationships. An element is an XML object that has a defined start and end tag, for example the start tag for an XML definition of a book could be <book>, and its subsequent end tag would then be </book>. An XML attribute is a name-value pair that modifies certain features of an element, for example a book could have "title" and "author" attributes.

Every element has to have a start and end tag in XML. If you are used to writing HTML, you might have become a bit lazy and used to missing out the end tags. For example, you might have used the <p>

element to start the first paragraph, and then used <p> again for the second paragraph - without putting a </p> end tag in between. HTML wouldn't care, however in XML if you did this you would have created an invalid document.

XML elements can be nested, for example a book obviously consists of a number of chapters, and therefore you might expect to see an XML document that represented this book similar to that shown in Listing 8.

```xml
<?xml version="1.0" encoding="UTF-8"?>
<!DOCTYPE book SYSTEM "book.dtd">
<book title="The Buildmeister's Guide">
    <preface>
    The preface ...
    </preface>
    <chapter title="Introduction" pages="5">
    In this chapter I will discuss …
    </chapter>
    <chapter title="Build Definitions" pages="8">
    Definitions are important ...
    </chapter>
    <index>
    Index ...
    </index>
</book>
```

Listing 8 – book.xml

This first line in this document states that it is an XML file and specifies what XML version it conforms to for compatibility purposes - expect to see a line similar to this in every XML document. The second line is a bit more interesting as it specifies the **Document Type Definition** (DTD). The DTD defines a "vocabulary" for the XML document, i.e., the elements, their attributes and relationships. The DTD for a generic book might look similar to that shown in Listing 9.

```
<!ELEMENT book (preface, chapter+, index)>
<!ELEMENT chapter (#PCDATA) …
<!ATTLIST book title CDATA #REQUIRED>
<!ATTLIST chapter title CDATA #REQUIRED pages CDATA ↩
#IMPLIED>

. . .
```

Listing 9 – book.dtd

This particular DTD defines that a book consists of three children: preface, chapter and index. They are all required and must be in this specific order. Also, you will notice that the chapter element on the first line has a "+" after it – which in regular expression speak means that the book has to have at least one chapter. The DTD also defines what attributes can be used for each of the elements. In this example line 4 defines that each chapter requires a "title" attribute but the (number of) "pages" attribute is optional. The #PCDATA (parsed character data) and CDATA keywords are simply used to specify that the content for an element or attribute is normal character text.

If you are using a tool which requires its input in XML, then you can examine its own DTD to see what the exact layout of the document should be. However, this is probably not the most accessible way of learning a tool and so the documentation for most usually presents the information in another way too. Where I believe that XML can become more useful in the build process however, is as an output format. If you are going to be creating any files during your build process, then create them in XML. Doing so, allows you to standardize your output, exchange information more easily between different tools, and present it as HTML - in different ways for different users. All of this can be carried via the use of XSLT technology, as I will discuss next. For more information on XML I recommend the first few chapters of *Beginning XML* [Hunter04].

XSLT

XSLT (XML Stylesheet Language Transformations) is a way of transforming the content of an existing XML document. Using XSLT you can transform the content of an XML document produced by one tool into a suitable format for use with another tool. You can also transform an XML formatted file into a HTML web page so that you can display it on a web-site.

To generate a HTML file from XML, you need to create an XSLT stylesheet file. Such a file contains the instructions for the transformation that you want to perform. XSLT stylesheets are built on structures called **templates**. A template specifies what to look for in a source tree (i.e., the XML input document) and what to output to the results tree (e.g., the HTML output document). An example for producing a summary of the book XML document created earlier is illustrated in Listing 10.

```
01:   <xsl:stylesheet version="1.0"
        xmlns:xsl="http://www.w3.org/1999/XSL/Transform">
02:   <xsl:output method="html"/>
03:   <xsl:variable name="startpage" select="1"/>
04:   <xsl:template match="book">
05:     <html>
06:     <body>
07:       <b>Summary of <xsl:value-of select="@title"/>
          </b>
08:       <br/>
09:       <xsl:apply-templates select="chapter"/>
10:       <b>Total Pages =
```

```
11:          <xsl:value-of select="sum(chapter/@pages)"/>
             </b>
12:      </body>
13:      </html>
14:   </xsl:template>
15:   <xsl:template match="chapter">
16:      Chapter <xsl:number value="position()"
         format="1 - "/>
17:      <xsl:value-of select="@title"/> has
18:      <xsl:value-of select="@pages"/> pages.
19:      <br/>
20:   </xsl:template>
21:   </xsl:stylesheet>
```

Listing 10 – book.xsl

Although Listing 10 looks quire complex, it is relatively straightforward to produce an XSLT file if you know the basics. The first thing that you will notice is that the example uses basic HTML formatting instructions, such as <body> and <b>, interspersed with XSLT formatting instructions (which all begin with "<xsl:"). You can transform an XML document to another XML document (for data integration purposes) but line 2 in this example is used to defined that the output of this translation will be pure HTML.

Line 3 in Listing 10 illustrates how you can define variables in XSL – in this case the variable startpage is set to the value "1". There are then two distinct "templates" in this example, the first on lines 4-13 which is used to summarize information on the book and the second on lines 15-20 which is used to display information about each of its chapters. Note that line 9 actually "calls" the chapter template using the <xsl:apply-templates> function. The rest of this example basically selects individual elements and attributes from the source document using the <xsl:value-of> function and **XPath** statements. XPath is a way of navigating the document hierarchy, for example to match the pages attribute of the `<chapter>` element the XPath "`chapter/@pages`" expression is used on line 11.

In order to apply an XSLT stylesheet to an XML document you will need an XSLT processor. There are a large number available, such as the open source tools **Saxon** (http://saxon.sourceforge.net), **Xalan-C++** (http://xml.apache.org/xalan-c) or the **Microsoft XML Core Services** (MSXML)[1]. Some build tools come will all the necessary libraries to carry out XSLT transformation, for example Apache Ant has an `<xslt>` task that can be used as in Listing 11.

```
<target name="transform">
    <xslt in="book.xml" out="book.html" style="book.xsl"/>
</target>
```

Listing 11 – Example Ant script to execute XSLT

If you executed this Ant script then you would produce a HTML file, which if opened in an Internet browser, would look something like the following:

```
Summary of The Buildmeister's Guide
Chapter 1 - Introduction has 5 pages.
Chapter 2 - Definitions has 8 pages. ...
Total Pages = 13
```

I believe there are many possibilities for using XML and XSLT within the build process, especially as a mechanism of producing reports and formatting their output for different users. In *IBM Rational ClearCase, Ant and CruiseControl* [Lee06] for example, I describe a detailed

---

[1] http://msdn2.microsoft.com/en-us/library/ms763742.aspx

example of how to automate the creation of baseline reports as a side affect of the build process. For more information on XSLT I recommend reading *XSLT For Dummies* [Wagner02].

Summary

There are no formal qualifications required for being a Buildmeister however I believe there are a set of core skills that every one should posses. Hopefully, by reading this chapter you will be encouraged to increase your own core skills and learn more about regular expressions, XML and XSLT and how they can be used in your own build process.

Once you have an understanding of what skills you require to implement a build process, the final piece is to physically implement the build process itself. In the next chapter I will look at a framework for implementing a build process and then at some best practices and guidelines to help you.

CHAPTER 6

Architecting Your Build Process

It is a safe rule to apply that, when a mathematical or philosophical author writes with a misty profundity, he is talking nonsense.
Alfred North Whitehead

When implementing any build process, it is important to understand what you want to achieve. This chapter introduces a high-level capability architecture for a typical build process and looks at the scope, decisions and issues that you should be aware of before implementation.

Build Capability Architecture

In order to implement any build process you must have some basic capabilities, usually a collection of hardware and tools, and some build scripts. However there are a number of additional capabilities that you can implement in an overall build process. A typical set of such capabilities are illustrated in Figure 12.

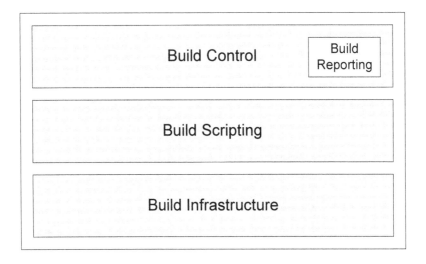

Figure 12 – Build Capabilities

The four capabilities in Figure 12 can be described in more detail as follows:

Build Infrastructure

A Build Infrastructure is the collective infrastructure that is required to support your build process, including the set of build and version control tools as well as the required, supporting hardware.

Build Scripting

Build Scripting is where build scripts (GNU Make, Apache Ant or other configuration scripts) are created. These scripts define how the different parts of the application should be compiled and/or linked together in order to produce a complete system or application. The scripts may also automate other parts of the process, for example, database configuration or installation. The scripting stage is where you define the guts of any automation that is to be carried out.

Build Control

Build Control is where the build scripts implemented in the Build Scripting phase are executed in a controlled (and sometimes automated) manner. Build Control also includes Build Reporting whereby the results of the build (success or failure) are reported on. There are many different types and levels of reporting: basic compilation reports, unit test reports, release reports and so on.

Breaking down the complete build process in this way allows you to concentrate on specific areas for implementation. For example, initially you might invest in a simple Build Infrastructure (a single server, open source tools) and a basic Build Scripting capability. Subsequently, you could then look at implementing a Build Control capability to automate and manage the execution of your build process. Finally, you could invest in a more comprehensive Build Infrastructure (multiple servers and commercial tools) as well as implementing a Build Reporting capability. These stages also align well to tools, for example Build Scripting can be carried out by tools such as GNU Make, Apache Ant or Microsoft MSBuild, whilst Build Control can be carried out by tools such as IBM Rational BuildForge, CruiseControl or Kinook Visual Build.

Project-level build capabilities

It is possible to share Build Infrastructure at the organizational level across many projects. However as discussed in chapters 3 and 4 build processes are ultimately implemented for each project environment. In order to help define what your project level build process should be, it is possible to define a number of additional project level build capabilities as illustrated in Figure 13.

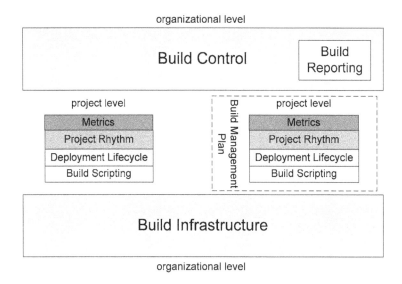

Figure 13 – Project-level Build Capabilities

This diagram is based on the set of build capabilities that were defined in Figure 12. However these capabilities are supplemented by an additional three project level capabilities, which can be summarised as follows:

Project Rhythm

A calculated definition of when, how and what a project should build. Finding your Project Rhythm is critical to understanding whether you have defined the right build process for your environment

Deployment Lifecycle

The defined execution lifecycle of the application being developed. This determines how the application is deployed to test and runtime environments and what infrastructure is required.

Build Metrics

A defined set of metrics that a project should capture on the execution of every build. Build Metrics are critical in understanding whether your build process is improving or degrading.

The main point of Figure 12 and Figure 13 is to provide a framework for assessing build process capability and to allow pertinent questions to be asked about any build process, for example:

- **Build Infrastructure** – what hardware infrastructure has been implemented to support the build process? What collection of tools is being used? Is the infrastructure being fully utilized? Can it be shared?

- **Build Scripting and Control** – how have build scripts been implemented? How are they executed? Are they secured?

- **Project Rhythm** – when and how often do you build? How long does a build take? Are you building regularly enough? Does your build take too long?

- **Deployment Lifecycle** – how is your application going to be deployed? Are you testing the deployment environment early enough? What infrastructure is required?

- **Build Metrics** – how many builds pass, how many fail? What software components are used in each build? Is the build success rate improving?

This is just a sample of the types of questions that can be asked, however it illustrates that by breaking down a build process into this capability architecture, you can start to understand more about the structure of your build process and the decisions that you will need to make. In the remainder of this chapter I will discuss these project level build capabilities in more detail.

Assess your Project Rhythm

For most projects knowing when to build and how often to build involves a fair bit of guesswork. For new projects builds are often executed on demand or maybe as part of a Daily Build process. However, do you know for a fact that this is the best or most appropriate build schedule? Are developers waiting for your builds, can your builds possibly be executed quicker?

In trying to answer these questions, you will probably find that your external release schedule is already defined by project and customer expectations, for example, an external release will be made once a quarter. However, internal to the project you will have much greater control over how changes are integrated and on what schedule. Note that there is no pre-defined schedule; you need to find the Project Rhythm that suits you best, by looking at patterns such as how long the build takes, how often developers can sensibly deliver and so on.

If you are adopting a Continuous Integration approach, this can mean building many times a day: maybe every 20 minutes or every hour. With more traditional forms of development this can mean building once a day (maybe as part of a nightly build). Your Project Rhythm will also be determined by any dependencies that exist between components or projects and how long the actual build process takes from beginning to end.

John Scumniotales[1] likens the different levels of a project's nested rhythms to a musical composition – an idea which is graphically illustrated in Figure 14.

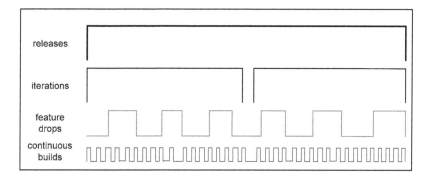

Figure 14 - Nested Rhythms

In such a scenario, the different rhythms act and interplay as follows:

- Continuous builds are the underlying beat, a metronome for Developers, setting the pace for code development, unit testing and integration.

- Feature Drops (or Milestone builds) are the metronome for Testers as they contain specific functionality for quality assurance.

- Iterations are the metronome for the Product Managers and the project as a whole as they provide high-level feedback on integration and usability.

- Finally Releases synchronize the interface with the Customer, aligning project planning and delivery dates.

---

[1] http://scrumone.typepad.com/agile_product_development/2006/06/rhythm_and_pace.html

The types of questions that you can ask to help determine your own Project Rhythm include the following:

- Are there any dependencies between internal components? If so, do the components have to be built in any specific order?

- Are there any dependencies on the output of external projects or components? If so, how will these outputs be made available?

- How many developers are working on the project? How often are they able to or expected to deliver changes into the integration area?

- What are the inputs for the developer's Private Builds? Will they build against the complete source code structure or against a partial structure and pre-built binaries from the Integration or Release Build?

- How often do testers expect or need an Integration Build for their own testing? What is the handover process?

- How long does it take to execute a full Integration or Release Build (including workspace population, compilation, unit-testing and internal deployment)?

- How often are Integration Builds expected to be carried out? Where will the outputs be stored?

- How often are Release Builds expected to be carried out? Where will the outputs be stored?

Although, this is not an exhaustive list of questions, if you can successfully answer just this set, then you should have enough information to be able to better understand when and what to build for your own project.

If you are the Buildmeister on a project, I recommend that you take a consultative approach by sitting down and discussing these questions with different members of your development team. Answering them will typically require some form of trade-off, e.g., the build could be carried out quicker but with more risk if a subset of unit tests were executed (at least during the day anyway). However, only by actively discussing and working through these decisions will you be confident that you are defining the right build process for your environment.

Define your Deployment Lifecycle

Perhaps the most fundamental question that you can ask yourself about your build process is what will the final output be? What is it you trying to create? At the end of the day, what you should be trying to produce is a self-contained, installable, documented and traceable release of software. This is often called the **Deployment Unit**, although this is not necessarily a single artifact like a J2EE ".ear" file, but rather a logical collection of related artifacts as is illustrated in Figure 15.

In Figure 15 you can see that the Deployment Unit consists of a number of artifacts at a number of levels. At the lowest level, your build "compilation" process is executed and a collection of **Deployment Component**(s) are produced; these are usually your built libraries (".jar", ".dll" files) or executables. The combination of all of the possible Deployment Components can be said to constitute your Release Build, which together with the **Release Note**(s) can be packaged up for ease of installation or deployment into a **Release Package**, for example a Windows Microsoft Installer (".msi") file. Finally, bringing all this together at the top level is the Deployment Unit itself which includes the Release Package as well as a **Bill of Materials** (detailing the contents on the Release Package) and **Supporting Artifacts** (such as Installation and Training documents).

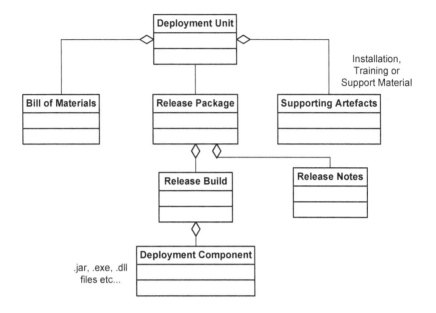

Figure 15 - Deployment Unit

In effect, a Deployment Unit is a reference to the set of files to be deployed, be they packaged up as part of a Release Package or simply the outputs of a Release Build. A Deployment Unit does not necessarily have to be a physical file, although it is certainly possible to create one - it could be a record and relationships in a database or a collection of links on a website. The important thing is that it contains everything that you need to be able to deploy and use an application.

Release Packages

The exact form that the Release Package part of the Deployment Unit takes and how it will be physically deployed will depend on the type of product that you are developing and the environment that you are deploying to. Table 2 lists a number of typical approaches.

Product Type	Release Package Format	Method of Deployment
Thick-client application Example: Microsoft Office.	Compressed file format, e.g. Zip file Self installing executable (".exe") Installation file, e.g. Microsoft ".msi", Redhat ".rpm" etc.	Simple file extraction External distribution via media (CD or DVD) External distribution via Internet download Internal distribution via tool, e.g. Microsoft Systems Manager Server
Thin-client web based application Example: Google Mail	Compressed file format, e.g. Zip file, Java Web Archive (".war")	Simple file copy or extraction Internal distribution via Intranet Internal distribution via Web server interface
Enterprise Application Example: Internet Banking application	J2EE Enterprise Archive file (.ear) including database, configuration and other supporting scripts.	Installation via command line or Web/Application Server user interface Programmatic installation via build scripting tool, e.g. Apache Ant, MSBuild
Firmware for consumer device Example: Cisco Router	Proprietary package format (usually binary)	External distribution via Internet download

Table 2 – Typical Deployment Approaches

The important point is that the release package should contain everything that it needs for it to be able to be deployed successfully. As an example, if you are creating an Enterprise Application that includes Web, database and messaging components, then you need to provide scripts (and instructions) to automate the installation and configuration of each of them.

Bill of Materials

The creation of an accessible, accurate and understandable Bill of Materials (BOM) is one of the most important responsibilities of the Buildmeister. The BOM details information on the build, what new features it contains, what defects it addresses and any extra installation or configuration steps that are required in order to get the build up and running. The information contained within it allows decisions to be made by the Test team on what (and what not to test). An example of such a document is illustrated Figure 16.

The BOM is primarily intended as an internal document and so can (and should) contain confidential, non-customer consumable information. However, a subset of the information contained in the BOM will usually be collated and presented in the form of a customer consumable release note. Since the BOM should be produced for every build (or at least every Feature Drop) it is important that its content is automated. Once of the best ways to do this is create an XML template for the BOM which is populated with information extracted from your Build, Version and Change Control tools at build time.

One of the more pragmatic ways of creating a BOM is to create and update a Build Wiki page that electronically represents it[2]. Such a Wiki page can be updated automatically on every build; it can also be commented on by users if they uncover important or additional information. Whatever mechanism you choose, creating a good BOM with up to date information should be one of your first tasks as a Buildmeister.

---

[2] www.buildmeister.com/kevinalee/downloads/update_build_wiki_0.1.zip illustrates how to achieve this using the Atlassian Confluence Wiki.

### *myReserve* Bill Of Materials	
Target Release: 1.1	**Date Created:** 12/12/08
Build Id: 012	**Created by:** Kevin Lee
Version Control Baseline: MR_1_1.012	
Install Location: \\share-01\myReserve\builds\MR_1_1.012	
Component Versions:	
CORE: 1.1 DB: 1.2.1 WEB: 1.3.1 ...	
Features Included:	
FEAT007: Find reservation by credit card FEAT012: Reserve multiple rooms FEAT016: Cancel reservation if more than 24 hours to arrival date ...	
Defects Addressed:	
DEF023: Can cancel a reservation if credit card is invalid DEF035: Searching for reservations with name containing hyphen causes error ...	
Installation Notes:	

Figure 16 - Example Bill Of Materials

Capture Build Metrics

Most people use the build process as a mechanism for capturing project code and test metrics; for example, when executing a build you might gather metrics on unit tests passed, code coverage or source lines of code (SLOC). However there are very few people who actually capture metrics on the build process itself.

For example, do you know how many of your builds have passed or failed and if your build success rate is improving? Metrics such as these can provide a valuable insight into how your project is progressing.

An example of the types of metrics that could be captured for the build processes are as follows:

- Number of passed or failed builds per project.
- Ratio of successful to failed builds.
- Average total build time per project build.
- Average time per individual build function.
- Number and name of components reused in a build.
- Number of change tasks and/or defects that have been implemented in each project build.

Some of these metrics will be easy to capture, some more difficult. In particular "Number and name of components reused in a build" is not a trivial metric to capture, however it could prove invaluable, especially if you are developing shared or reusable components. If you are able to demonstrate how components have been reused, then this will go a long way to help in justifying the cost of preparing and packaging other components for subsequent reuse.

I'm sure there are a number of other build process metrics that you could think of. However, the point with any set of metrics is to define a small set, automate their capture, and make them visible to all members of your team. If people are used to seeing certain metrics then it gets much easier to be able to recognize trends or bad "smells" in your projects. One you have seen a trend then you can be proactive and start doing something about it.

Create a Build Management Plan

To formalize the decisions and tradeoffs that you make when defining your project-specific build and deployment process, you can create a

Build Management Plan. This is a document similar in structure to a Software Configuration Management Plan[3] but concentrates specifically on build and deployment issues by defining:

- Build team organization and responsibilities.
- Build tools, environment and infrastructure.
- Build activities, including identification and control mechanisms.
- Build accounting, including metrics, reporting and auditing.

As with any document, I believe the process of understanding – identifying important decisions and making them – is just as important as the creation of the final document itself. Consequently, you should capture and document your Build Management Plan in whatever format you deem suitable, for example a Wiki page or a Microsoft Word document. An example of a Build Management Plan for an application called *MyReserve*[4] is illustrated in Appendix B.

Summary

There are a number of important decisions that need to be made when defining any build and deployment process. This chapter has looked at the build process from an architectural point of view in order to establish what the different constituent parts of a build process are. I believe that by doing so you should now have an understanding of your own build capability and what you need to do to refine or improve it.

---

[3] See www.sei.cmu.edu/legacy/scm/abstracts/abscm_plans.html for more information on SCM plans.
[4] http://myreserve.sourceforge.net

With this architecture in mind, in the next chapter I will move on to the physical implementation of the build process itself and define a number of reuseable "good" practices.

Implementing your Build Process

The world is moving so fast these days that the man who says it can't be done is generally interrupted by someone doing it.
Harry Emerson Fosdick

At some stage you will either need to physically implement a new build process or refine an existing one. This chapter describes a number of patterns and techniques for implementing a build process.

Implementing your Build Infrastructure

Build Infrastructure is the collective infrastructure that is required to support your build process, including the set of build and version control tool as well as the required, supporting hardware. In this section I will look at how best to implement and make use of your Build Infrastructure.

Implement shared hardware

In chapter 2 I discussed the typical server components of a Build Infrastructure. Implementing and administering such an infrastructure can be costly and time consuming for an individual project. One of questions you should ask yourself is, are you "reinventing the wheel" for each project? Instead, could you consolidate and reuse a single hardware infrastructure across many projects?

From an organizational point of view it makes sense to consolidate and share infrastructure across many projects. If your organization already has a central or virtual development tools team, then such consolidation should be relatively straightforward to agree, implement and administer. However, one of the concerns of such an implementation for an individual project is ensuring that sufficient resource is reserved for them. With shared servers there is obviously the potential that other unrelated projects have already "loaded" the build infrastructure. In order to mitigate against this you can adopt one of two strategies:

Implement consolidation at the business unit level.
Although some organizations might agree with the concept of build infrastructure consolidation they prefer to implement it at the organizational or business unit level. By doing so they ensure that any resources are at least being utilised by the same nominal cost centre.

Implement a mixture of dedicated and shared infrastructure.
In order to guarantee that a minimum amount of build servers are available you can allocate one or more dedicated servers to a project. When you subsequently execute a build, it will be executed on these servers first and then check the shared pool of servers to see if other resources are available. If so the build load will be spread to these servers thus reducing total build time.

Note that in order to be able to implement these techniques you will need access to technology that manages load balancing and sharing across servers. There are many hardware and software solutions to achieve this as well as build specific solutions like **IBM Rational BuildForge** (www.buildforge.com) or **Electric Cloud ElectricAccelerator** (www.electric-cloud.com).

As well as consolidating the actual build server infrastructure, it can also be cost effective to consolidate build server tools – specifically their installation and support. However, since build processes are project-specific you will need to ensure that project's do have sufficient access rights to the tools themselves.

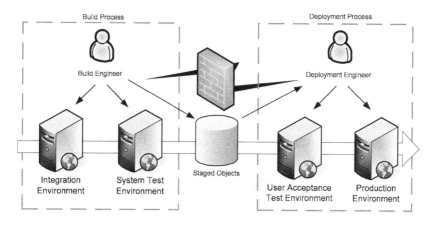

Figure 17 - Deployment Lifecycle

Manage your Deployment Environments

All applications go through a number of stages in a deployment lifecycle, typically from development to test and then into production (where production can be release to manufacturing or installation in a physical hardware environment). An example of a typical deployment lifecycle is illustrated in Figure 17.

For thick-client or consumer device applications, this deployment lifecycle is usually relatively straightforward. However where applications are being deployed to server based environments, such as with Web based or Enterprise applications this can be a very complex and time consuming exercise. This is typically because there are multiple servers in each environment, each of which needs to be installed, configured and tested before the application can be executed.

In most organizations, deployment will be made to a variation of the Development, System Test, User Acceptance Test and Production deployment lifecycle. In an ideal situation, the deployment lifecycle would simply iterate the same process for each of these environments over and over again, with the level of approval required being dependent on the environment that was being deployed to. Unfortunately however this is not always possible as there are often different numbers or variations of servers in each environment and different environments are often managed by different departments (as illustrated in Figure 17). Given this situation it is important that the deployment process is automated and controlled and verified as early and as much as possible.

Hopefully, your application will always deploy successfully, but what happens if this is not the case? Similarly, what happens if the application fails on deployment (maybe because of insufficient integration or defective implementation)? You might be able to get away with this in development and test environments – indeed it might be somewhat expected. However, in Production this is clearly not acceptable. For all releases that are to be deployed to Production environments you should always have a **back-out plan** and test it.

For example, if you deploy a new release onto the Production servers and subsequently find that there are problems with it, there should be a process in place for removing this release and rolling back to the previous one. In such a scenario it is desirable that this process is as automatic as possible.

Purchasing physical hardware for each of your deployment environments can be a significant cost. Not only in terms of the cost of the hardware but in terms of the management of it as well. One approach that is being used more often is the virtualization of hardware using software technology such as **VMWare ESX Server**[1] or **Microsoft Virtual Server**[2]. You can use virtualization for any environment, but it is particularly useful for the creation of a **virtual lab** of the development and testing environments – where different operating systems and applications new to be provisioned frequently and rapidly.

As an example, if a problem is found in Production then this environment needs to be rapidly created so that the problem can be reproduced. One way of achieving this is to create a library of virtual machines and store them in a repository – maybe your version control system if it has good support for large binaries. When you subsequently need to create a fix, you can "checkout" not only the baseline of the code that you need to fix but also the environment that you need to reproduce and execute it on[3].

Select appropriate tools

I do not believe it is possible to implement a comprehensive end-to-end build and deployment process by using a single tool. Instead, I believe a combination of related and integrated tools are required. Unfortunately, there are a vast array of tools – both open source and commercial – that fit in the build process space. As an example, try carrying out a search on Google for "build automation". I recommend selecting and implementing tools in three different phases as follows:

---

[1] www.vmware.com/products/vi/esx/
[2] www.microsoft.com/windowsserversystem/virtualserver/
[3] VMware Lab Manager (www.vmware.com/products/labmanager/) offers a comprehensive approach to managing your virtual lab.

- Select a **Build Scripting** tool that is most appropriate for your implementation environment.

- Select a deployment tool or approach that automates and manages the deployment of your application.

- Select a **Build Control** tool that allows you to manage, distribute and automate the execution of your builds as required by your Project Rhythm.

Build Scripting tools allow you to script up your build process, calling compilers, unit test tools and packaging commands as and when required. To some degree your choice of a Build Scripting tool will already be dictated to you by your environment as I discussed in chapter 3. However, there are also other tools where no scripting is required and you use a GUI to define your build process based on pre-defined libraries of build actions or routines, examples include **OpenMake's Meister** (www.openmake.com), and **VSoft's FinalBuilder** (www.finalbuilder.com).

Whether you actually need a specific deployment tool will depend on the complexity of your deployment approach. Often you can use your Build Scripting tool to automate deployment, however sometimes because of the complexity of the environment you can save a significant amount of time by using virtualization technologies or specific deployment and provisioning software such as (the built-in build and deployment capabilities of) **Serena Dimensions** (www.serena.com/products/dimensions/) **Tivoli Provisioning Manager** (www.ibm.com/software/tivoli/products/prov-mgr/) or **BladeLogic Configuration Manager** (www.bladelogic.com)[4].

To identify your Build Control tool you should look at your Project Rhythm and select a tool that most appropriately supports it.

---

[4] Note that some of these tools are Enterprise class with high-end prices and are typically purchased to manage Production data centre environments.

There are many such tools and they are described slightly differently depending on their capabilities, for example: "Continuous Integration Server", "Build Management Server", or "Build and Release Framework", however at the lowest level they all carry out a similar job of executing pre-defined commands or scripts. Some well known examples of Build Control tools include **IBM Rational BuildForge** (www.ibm.com/software/awdtools/buildforge), the open source **CruiseControl** tool (http://cruisecontrol.sourceforge.net) and **Anthill Professional** tool (www.urbancode.com).

One of the main decisions in selecting a Build Control tool is deciding whether you are simply selecting a tool for a specific project or whether you are selecting a tool to meet the requirements of many different projects, potentially implementing different technologies and working in different environments. The difference between these two decisions tends to be reflected in whether it is an open source or commercial tool. As soon as you start talking about an organizational tool, you are inevitably going to require scalability, configurability and support - something which you usually have to pay for.

Selecting a tool for an Enterprise is often fraught with politics, emotions and is most of the time quite difficult. There is also a lot to be said for selecting a tool without all of the bells and whistles but that meets a core set of requirements - which is the preferred approach of Agilists. To help you to decide which type of Build Control tool is appropriate, I have listed a set of basic requirements in Appendix A.

Create a standard build structure

If you are going to build multiple projects or applications you should agree on a standard directory structure and document it – probably in your Build Management Plan. This should include all aspects of the build process such as where the source and test components will reside, where the build outputs will be created, what the build scripts should be called and so on.

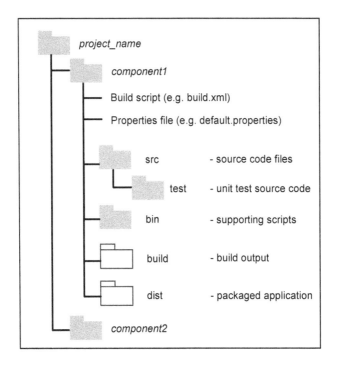

Figure 18 - Example Build Directory Structure

An example of a standard project directory structure for building an application can be seen in Figure 18. Obviously the contents and layout of this directory structure will vary slightly, depending on the "type" of application that you are developing, but you should at least try and stick to common names. For example irrespective of whether you are creating a Java or Microsoft.NET component I would recommend that source code is held in a `src` directory and compiled objects written to a `build` directory. Note that the actual names are not as important as the fact that you are being consistent.

When you are executing a full Integration or Release Build, you should do so in a clean and controlled environment. The best way to achieve this is to create a dedicated build workspace – a file system directory populated from your version control repository. This workspace should be synchronised with the development environment before building. This can be to either the latest set of development changes (for an Integration Build) or to a specific baseline (for a Release Build). You should use different build workspace for different releases of your projects or applications.

Most version control tools have a capability to create complete workspaces, for example in CVS or Subversion it is explicitly called a workspace, in Serena Dimensions CM it is called a work area whilst in IBM Rational ClearCase a workspace is realized by a ClearCase View.

Implementing Build Scripting

In order to execute your build process you will need to implement scripts. These scripts are usually in one of the following two categories:

- **Build scripts** – scripts that are created as an input to some build tool, such as Apache Ant or GNU Make.

- **Command scripts** – controlling or sub-scripts which acts as wrappers or carry out more logical or data based manipulation. Command scripts are typically written in an interpreted or scripting language such as Perl, Python, VBScript, Ruby or Linux/UNIX shell script.

How much scripting you need to carry out depends on the tools that you choose, for example Apache Ant and GNU Make require a significant amount of build scripting, whilst the Microsoft Visual Studio.NET can generate and edit MSBuild scripts directly from the IDE. There are also high-level build framework tools such as OpenMake which are GUI driven and generate a significant amount of the build scripts for you behind the scenes. I believe however that any reasonable build process will include some form of build or command scripting. The rest of this section describes some strategies for implementing build and command scripts.

Create reuseable build scripts

One of the most important practices in software development is reuse. If implemented correctly, reuse can help save time and effort as well as ensure consistency and reliability. In chapter 2, I discussed the concept of a RADICAL build process, well exactly the same concepts apply to the scripts that you are creating to implement your process. If you have a project containing multiple components or many projects implemented in the same language it will be certainly worth your time ensuring that your build scripts are reuseable.

Most build scripting tools have the ability to "import" the contents of one file into another. This capability can allow you to create a library of reuseable routines and then import them into a coordinating build script. As an example, if you were using MSBuild you could create a project build script that contained common targets similar to Listing 12.

```xml
<?xml version="1.0" encoding="utf-8" ?>
<Project xmlns="http://schemas.microsoft.com/
     developer/msbuild/2003">

   <PropertyGroup>
      <Configuration Condition=" '$(Configuration)' ↩
         == '' ">Debug</Configuration>
   </PropertyGroup>

   <Target Name="Compile">
      <Csc Sources="@(SourceFiles)"
         OutputAssembly="$(appname).exe"/>
   </Target>
```

```
</Project>
```

Listing 12 – Common.targets

This example defines a common "Compile" target with parameters. This file can then simply be imported and its targets reused as illustrated in Listing 13.

```
<Project DefaultTargets="Compile"
    xmlns="http://schemas.microsoft.com/
    developer/msbuild/2003">
    <PropertyGroup>
        <Configuration>Release</Configuration>
    </PropertyGroup>
    <ItemGroup>
        <SourceFiles Include="*.cs"/>
    </ItemGroup>
    <Import Project="Common.targets"/>
</Project>
```

Listing 13 – MSBuild script using Common.targets

Apache Ant has a similar capability, where you can import a common build script as follows:

```
<import file="common.targets" optional="false"/>
```

GNU Make has the import function that was used in chapter 5, Listing 2.

Manage build configuration

Rather than specifying configuration parameters directly in your build scripts, you should move their definition out to specific property files. This effectively separates your control logic from your data, applying a Model-View-Controller[5] (MVC) like design pattern. For example, instead of hard-coding values in your scripts such as directory names, environment variables and debugging parameters, place them in separate configuration files. As an example, with Apache Ant you can create a file called `default.properties` that resides alongside your build script and had content similar to the following:

```
#default.properties
compile.debug = false
compile.compiler = javac1.4
repository = myreserve
build.admin = Kevin
```

You could then import the contents of this file using the `<property>` task at the top of your build script, as follows:

```
<property file="default.properties"/>
```

These properties can now be edited from once central place, or alternately passed via the command line for build specific settings. In MSBuild you can achieve the same result by using the element:

```
<Import Project="filename"/>
```

This was described and illustrated in Listing 12 and Listing 13. With GNU Make you can use of the similar `import` function.

---

[5] http://java.sun.com/blueprints/patterns/MVC.html

Manage deployment configuration

One of the main issues you will probably encounter with the deployment process is how to cater for deployment configuration. In such a context, configuration involves changing parameters to define how the application executes in different environments. For example, you will certainly have different server names, database and message queue configurations in your Development environment compared to your Production environments. Such parameters are usually contained in distinct property or configuration files and should be part of the Deployment Unit. If at all possible you should implement your application so that it is configurable "on-the-fly", this means that parameters can be changed in a file, which the application monitors, and on a change automatically re-initializes itself. However this is not always possible.

I have often seen organizations develop an application without consideration for how it needs to be configured in each environment. A few times the application has proven too difficult to configure and consequently some additional functionality implemented to ease this process. When designing or architecting your application it is important that you define a strategy on how configuration is handled and implement it early. Example strategies include creating a new Deployment Unit configured for each environment or providing application functionality and scripts that extract configuration parameters and re-initialise the application accordingly.

A simple approach to building for or deploying to different environments can be implemented using Apache Ant or MSBuild properties and conditional logic. For example Listing 14 illustrates how an application could be packaged for two different environments: Development and System Test, using MSBuild properties and conditions.

```
<Project xmlns="http://schemas.microsoft.com/developer/
```

```
  msbuild/2003" DefaultTargets="Dist">

 <PropertyGroup>
   <Environment Condition=" '$(Environment)' ==
     '' ">Development</Environment>
 </PropertyGroup>

 <PropertyGroup Condition=" '$(Environment)'==
   'Development'">
   <ServerName>devserver</ServerName>
 </PropertyGroup>

 <PropertyGroup Condition=" '$(Environment)' ==
   'SystemTest' ">
   <ServerName>testserver</ServerName>
 </PropertyGroup>

 <Target Name="PackageForDev" Condition="'$(Environment)'
   == 'Development'">
   <Message Text="Executing Development packaging..."/>
 </Target>

 <Target Name="PackageForTest"
   Condition="'$(Environment)' == 'SystemTest'">
   <Message Text="Executing SystemTest packaging..."/>
 </Target>

 <Target Name="Dist"
   DependsOnTargets="PackageForDev;PackageForTest">
   <Message Text="Deploying to server = $(ServerName)"/>
 </Target>

</Project>
```

Listing 14 – Deployment configuration script

An example of using this build script from the command line to create a package for the "SystemTest" environment would be as follows:

```
msbuild /t:Dist /p:Environment=SystemTest
```

A similar approach can be achieved in Apache Ant using the "if" and "unless" attributes for a target, for example:

```
<target name="PackageForTest" if="SystemTest">
```

Ant also has a <condition> task which can set a property based on a collection of possible conditions, for example, whether another property is set, whether a file exists on disk and so on[6]. Note that properties and conditional targets in Ant are not as flexible as MSBuild, in the above example it is not possible to check for the "value" of the SystemTest property in the above rather only that it has been set to a specific value.

As well as executing specific actions in a target, you can also make use of template files and search and replace functionality within your build scripts. For example, if you were developing an application which used a database, rather than hard coding the database parameters within your application you could define placeholders similar to the following:

```
define("DB_SERVER", "@db_server@");
define("DB_USER", "@db_user@");
define("DB_PASS", "@db_pass@");
define("DB_NAME", "@db_name@");
```

You could then, use your build scripting tool to search and replace the value of these strings dependent upon which environment you were

---

[6] See [LEEABM07] for examples on how to use the <condition> task.

deploying to. An example of an Apache Ant target to achieve this is illustrated in Listing 15.

```
<target name="deploy2prod" if="env.prod">
    <property file="prod.properties"/>
    <copy overwrite="true"
     file="template_constants.php"
     tofile="constants.php"/>
    <replace file="include/constants.php"
     propertyfile="prod.properties">
        <replacefilter token="@db_server@"
         property="db.server"/>
        <replacefilter token="@db_user@"
         property="db.user"/>
        . . .
    </replace>
</target>
```

Listing 15 – Deployment search and replace script

In this example, the "deploy2dev" target will only be executed if the "env.prod" property is set. If it is, then a template file containing the placeholder strings ("template_constants.java") is copied over to the file to be built and deployed ("constants.java"). The Ant <replace> task is then used to load the values of the properties from an environment specific property file ("prod.properties"), and replace the placeholder strings. Similar tasks are available in GNU Make and MSBuild (using the MSBuild community tasks[7]).

Note that some implementation environments also allow you to specify logical parameters that are mapped to physical parameters at

---

[7] http://msbuildtasks.tigris.org/

deployment time. For example, the J2EE specification allows you to specify security "roles" (in an applications deployment descriptor[8]) for its pages and components. This would allow you to define an "admin" role that could only access administration pages as an example. When the application is deployed to an Application Server you can then map this role to a physical role such as a corporate Windows Active Directory group. This can either be done manually using the Application Server's management console or through scripting to automate the process.

Implement build functions incrementally

In chapter 2, I defined a comprehensive set of possible build functions, e.g., Compilation, Unit Testing, Packaging and so on. You do not have to implement all of these build functions, however there is usually a minimal set of functions that will need to be implemented in your build scripts for them to be "useful". The rest of the build functions can be implemented over time, which gives you the ability to plan and increase your build capability incrementally.

Note that implementing a build function means that it is an automated and intrinsic part of your overall build process, not something you execute separately or manually. There is little point in creating a wide-ranging and functionally rich build process if it consists of many manual and error prone steps.

Manage product variants at build and runtime

In many organizations, products are developed to meet the needs of multiple customers, markets or environments. For example, Financial Services trading systems are amended with new business rules for each

---

[8] See www.buildmeister.com/viewarticle.php?id=2 for more information on J2EE packaging and deployment

international market into which they are deployed. In these types of products there is usually a significant amount of common, reusable code with a smaller subset that needs to be changed for each customer, market or environment. The end result is the creation of a number of different but ultimately related products which are usually termed product **variants**.

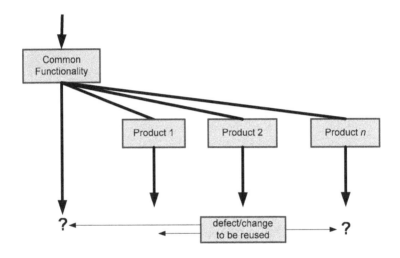

Figure 19 - Product variant development using branches

It has been common to manage the development of such variants using long lived version control branches as illustrated in Figure 19. In this example a large number of product variants are being developed – which can quickly lead to an explosion in the number of branches. Any defects or changes made to the individual products needs to be carefully assessed; if they affect multiple products then frequent and complex merges might be required. At the feature level, most version control and SCM tools are quite capable of supporting such strategies. However it should be remembered that whenever you branch, at some stage a subsequent merge will be required. Most non-trivial merges require human intervention, and as we know with any human based operation, errors can be made. There is therefore inevitably a degree of risk associated with such strategies. It is now widely accepted by the software development industry that managing product variants solely by branching alone is insufficient[9]. Indeed, I have personally witnessed the failure of such implementations (usually in terms of failure to integrate successfully and deliver on time) on a number of projects.

An alternative method of managing the creation of product variants is to develop a single codeline (with limited branching[10]) that can be configured or tailored at build or runtime to include specific variant features. There are typically three mechanisms that can be used to achieve this which can be summarized as follows:

- **compile-time variation** – where source code features are developed and conditionally "compiled in" using pre-processor "#ifdef" style statements. This is a simple strategy to implement but can quite quickly cause untestable spaghetti style code. See Henry Spencer's article *"#ifdef Considered Harmful"* [Spencer92] for a discussion on how bad practices using "#ifdef" statements can evolve.

- **link-time variation** – where feature code is firstly developed as abstract interfaces and then the object modules that realize them are selected and bound at build link-time.

- **run-time variation** – where the entire set of customer, market and potentially environmental

---

[9] www.bcs-cmsg.org.uk/conference/2007/papers/dalgarno.pdf
[10] You might still use branches for managing concurrent releases, maintenance fixes and maybe even feature development for complex environments.

features is developed and included in a product but can be "configured" to be available at run-time. This is usually achieved through the use of configuration files, licensing or some other similar mechanism.

Whichever mechanism you choose, your build and deployment process will need to be designed to support it from the beginning. For example, if you are implementing compile-time variation then you need to make sure that the relevant flags can be passed to your compiler, and that they can be recorded and controlled via your build scripts (see "*Manage build configuration*" above for an example). If you are implementing link-time variation then you need to ensure that have an appropriate directory structure (see "*Create a standard directory structure*" above) and that your build process can be configured to select from within this directory structure the appropriate modules for a specific variant. Finally, for run-time variation you need to ensure that your deployment and installation process is suitable documented (see "*Manage deployment configuration*") and has been rigorously tested for run-time configuration.

For further discussions on the application of build and deploy time variants, see Dalgarno and Beuche's paper on *Variant Management* [Dalgarno07] and Sukanen's thesis *Extension Frameworks for Symbian OS applications* [Sukanen04].

Document and manage your build scripts

Most developers agree on the benefits of documenting their source code so that it can be maintained over time[11]. Your build scripts should be treated no differently. All build scripting tools allow you to incorporate comments in your scripts; some also allow you to describe the process or targets that you are creating. As an example, Apache

Ant allows each of its targets to be "described" using an attribute as in the following:

```
<target name="clean"
    description="remove generated files">
    <!-- remove directory structure -->
    ...
<target name="compile"
    description="compile all source code">
...
```

The advantage of the Ant approach is that you can execute "ant -p" from the command line to print a list of all of the targets in the build script, along with their descriptions:

```
>ant -p
Buildfile: build.xml
Main targets:
    clean:          remove generated files
    compile:        compile all source code
...
```

Neither MSBuild nor GNU Make has similar attributes, but you can use equivalent comments instead.

As well as documenting your build scripts, I also find it useful to create a workflow diagram or dependency graph of the process being implemented in the collection of build scripts. This is especially important where you have multiple components and are using common or reuseable routines. As an example Figure 20, illustrates a dependency diagram for an MSBuild project.

---

[11] Some even carry it out!

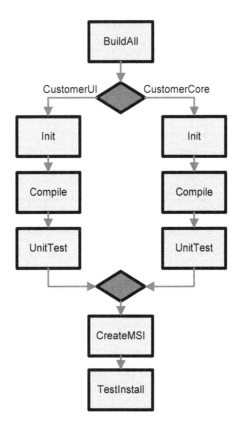

Figure 20 – Example MSBuild dependency diagram

You could publish such a diagram on your Intranet or Wiki for users to examine. In the past I have published diagrams such as these and created web "hotspots" on each of the targets so that if the users hover over or click on them, they are presented with a brief explanation.

Unfortunately, static diagrams such as these can often quickly out of date – especially if a build process is still evolving. There are a number of tools you can use to generate diagrams similar to Figure 20 (some even allow you to do it automatically as part of your build process). Examples include **Grand** (www.ggtools.net/grand) for

Apache   Ant   build   scripts   and   **MSBuild   Sidekick** (www.attrice.info/msbuild/index.htm) for MSBuild.

Implementing Build Control

Once you have a core set of build scripts you can start to actively organize and manage their execution. This is where the implementation of a well designed Build Control capability can start to add significant value. The rest of this section describes some strategies for implementing Build Control.

Automate only what you need to

There is a common misconception in software development that automation is good and everything that possibly can be automated should be. Although this is true to a degree, automating everything does take time and the question that you need to ask yourself is how often is the task that you are automating going to be run. If it is going to be run 100 times, then great the effort of automating it will be worth it; however, if it is going to be run just two or three times then is the level of investment in automation really worth it?

As an example for build functions take the Deployment function. If you have a complex deployment process that requires an application to be installed in many different environments then it is essential to script it. However if your deployment process is simply the installation of a pre-packaged application - such as a Windows install file - then you should probably not spend too much time worrying about how to automate its deployment, and instead let users (such as testers) browse to a known location and install it themselves.

Decompose your build process

Usually, there are many areas of your build process where you could save execution time by running different, unrelated parts in parallel. Often however it is difficult to visualize how this would be possible and where the dependencies would be. The best way of assessing what you could execute in parallel is to look at your Project Rhythm and decompose the execution of your overall build process as follows:

- **Component level** - identify which individual projects or components can be executed in parallel and which have to be built in a specific order.

- **Function level** – identify what build functions can be executed in parallel for each component, for example compilation and generating documentation.

When you have decomposed your build process in such a way, you can then either script its execution or used a Build Control tool that supports parallel processing.

Implement discrete build and deployment scenarios

Once you have decomposed your build process you can then identify a number of common scenarios which you would expect to execute. In an ideal world you would execute your complete build and deployment process from beginning to end, however in reality it is more likely that you will need to execute discrete parts of your overall process. For example, if you are fixing a problem in a component of your overall application – you would want to "rebuild" just that component. Similarly you might have different sets of users that need to execute your "build" process as opposed to your "deployment" process. An example of related build and deployment scenarios is illustrated in Figure 21. Note that this example also illustrates build functions (`Compile` and `DocGen` for "`Component1`") being executed in parallel.

The important point is that each of these distinct scenarios should call the same build scripts, but via a different entry point. It can help significantly if this different entry points are presented visually (usually as discrete projects) in a Build Control tool such as CruiseControl or IBM Rational Build Forge.

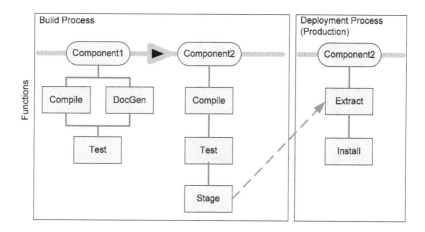

Figure 21 – Example build and deployment decomposition

Rebuild only if necessary

Often software development teams build everything - the complete code base - at each build. This obviously means that each build will take a predictable but maximum amount of time. Although such a process might still be desired for Release Builds - when you are deploying the build to external customers - for ongoing development and integration purposes this can cause significantly project delays. Consequently, if possible I prefer to carry out a full rebuild only if strictly necessary. If a component has not changed then consume the previous built version rather than re-building it.

Your customers will often make you do this too. Although you might feel that it is as quick and more reliable to do a complete build, try giving a complete set of re-built binaries to a customer when only a minor change has been made!

Execute unit testing in phases

If you have a comprehensive suite of unit tests then executing the complete suite may take a significant amount of time and increase the total build time. One of the ways to mitigate this is to execute unit testing in phases, for example you could execute a core set of unit tests during the day (usually as part of a Continuous Integration build) so that developers can gain essential feedback, and then execute the complete suite of tests overnight.

Note that following this technique (as well as the partial build technique) can introduce a degree of risk, however I believe that this risk is worth taking in the short term in order to rapidly progress an Agile Software Delivery approach.

Create a build pipeline

In order to be able to consume previously built projects and components you can create a **build pipeline.** Rather than a Continuous Integration approach of monitoring source code and initiating a build on changes, a build pipeline monitors a **binary repository** for staged build outputs[12]. An example of a build pipeline is illustrated in Figure 22. In this example a number of builds (but with partial testing) are first carried out by Project 1. At some stage (probably overnight) a complete build, including full testing, deployment and staging is carried out by Project 1. This is used a trigger for Project 2's build to

---

[12] As a result this approach is sometimes referred to as Continuous Staging.

start. Obviously change in the source code for Project 2 will also trigger a build.

In a similar vein, a number of Build Control tools allow you to create dependencies between build projects. In this way if a project is built successfully then another project can be started. However this approach would consume all the binary outputs of the first project rather than just the ones that had changed.

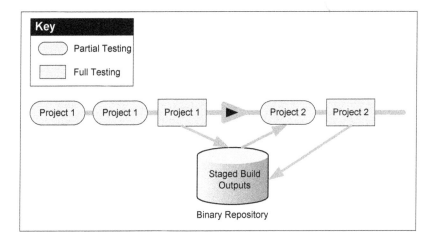

Figure 22 – Example build pipeline

Secure and audit your deployment process

In chapter 6 I described a typical deployment lifecycle, moving from Development through to Production. I would expect any build process to automatically deployment to Development and maybe System Test environments. However for User Acceptance Test and Production Environments, I would expect the deployment process to be more controlled and secure.

The best way of achieving this is to create distinct process in your Build Control tool (as discussed earlier) and to prompt for and request any usernames and passwords that are required for access to servers (e.g. Web or Application Servers). Typically you can hardcode the usernames and passwords for the Development and maybe Test environments, but make sure that these usernames fail for the Production environment.

Whenever any deployment process is invoked you should also audit the fact that it has happened, what has been deployed and who initiated it. This information can be vital in helping you solve problems and ensure that you are meeting any compliance mandates.

Summary

Software development is still more of an art than a science, and this is particularly true with the definition and implementation of build processes. Hopefully, by following some of the guidelines and practices in this section you can start to subjectively discuss the relative merits of different build processes and have some idea about how good your own build process is and what steps you can take to make it better.

Epilogue

If it weren't for the last minute, nothing would get done
Anonymous

In my opinion, a large number of software development organizations still do not systematically implement their build processes. Instead they usually create them in an ad hoc fashion, and evolve them as needed with limited effort and resources. Consequently, their build processes tend to go "stale" very quickly. They often remain untouched, either because no one can understand them or because it is deemed too risky to change them. When existing build processes are not documented or well understood, rather than make incremental changes, I have often seen organizations discard their complete build process and implement a new one from scratch.

In a large number of projects, the only time that a build process will be changed is when it fundamentally has to. This is usually on certain key events such as:

- the initiation of a new project,
- a fundamental change in system architecture,

- a need to increase a project's delivery rate,
- or a requirement to conform to some new regulatory compliance mandate

If there is a dedicated Buildmeister involved in defining the build process, then they will usually implement it based on past experience or instinct. Although some guidance on implementing build tools can be found in books and on the Internet, there is very little guidance and information on how to implement a generic build process – something which hopefully this book now covers. Whatever the reason for creating or changing a build process, it can be very difficult to know where to start or how to systematically assess the capability of your current build process.

Perhaps the most interesting and fun aspect of implementing a build process is learning new technology and tools. The nature of software development is that there will always be another new tool to use; and often there is often an assumption that by implementing them you will automatically gain a better build process. I hope by now that you agree with me that this is hardly ever true.

Instead I believe you should look at your overall build process capability: what does your build process need to do, how can it be improved and what is the best way of structuring its implementation. I have consciously tried to concentrate this book on process first – although the tools will always find a way to creep in at some stage. The Build Capability Architecture I introduced in chapter 6 abstracts a lot of what I believe the build process is intended to achieve and hopefully raises the level of maturity for a discipline which is still in its infancy.

Making the change

If you are a Buildmeister working on a development project then hopefully reading this book has empowered you with ideas about how to implement or improve your own build process. However, in software development we can't always do the things that we want. If you are going to implement something new or change something that is already in existence, you will probably need to ensure that you have buy-in from your development team and your management.

Winning over developers can usually be done by discussing the technical facts. Tell them what you want to implement, how it will make their lives easier and maybe even what "fancy" technology you are going to use. They will usually understand what is in it for them. They might even be the catalysts for change themselves. Winning over management can be somewhat trickier. Why should they approve a change to something that they can't understand or don't believe is broken? Fortunately, there are a few things you can do to help with this:

Establish a baseline of your current process.

You can baseline your current process by capturing some basic Build Metrics, e.g., how long builds take, the amount that fail. Use these metrics to help illustrate the current situation and where these is room for improvement. Estimate what implementing a new build process could achieve. Obviously, don't go too wild in estimating though as you will be expected to deliver on it.

Research and communicate industry best practices.

Change will be a lot easier for management to agree to if there are recognised industry benefits. Hopefully, this book can help with this[1]. However, there are also analyst reports, such as those by **Gartner** (www.gartner.com) and **Forrester** (www.forrester.com) that talk about build and release management industry best practices and tools.

Create a Build Management Plan.

If you want to systematically improve the capability and maturity of your build process, I recommend taking the time to create a Build Management Plan based on the template in Appendix B. Remember though it is not so much the documented end result that is important, more the process of identifying solutions and making considered decisions.

Whatever mechanism you choose to get the go ahead, make sure you capture and report on any incremental improvement. If you receive positive feedback from a developer, tester or internal customer, which you can say is down to the result of a change you made in the build process, then communicate it. Also, keep tracking those Build Metrics. People like to see trends; even if things go bad for a short while (as they might do when you try something new), if you can demonstrate a history of turning things around, then it will be much easier for people to accept.

Additional resources

There is a wealth of content and information about the build process available on the Internet. Unfortunately, quite a lot of it is tied in with commercial vendor tools – always look at best practice documents from commercial vendors carefully. However, here are some recommended websites which you can use to help you in your research.

---

[1] Please feel free to purchase a copy for your Manager!

www.buildmeister.com

The Buildmeister website is a portal created by myself for documenting best practices and tools for the build process. You will find information that was used as the background for this book as well as more in depth discussions on build tools.

www.cmcrossroads.com

CM Crossroads is the configuration management community online. It hosts lots of articles, product reviews, webcasts and discussion forums. Although about configuration management in general it does have some areas dedicated to software build and release management.

www.bcs-cmsg.org.uk

The **British Computer Society Configuration Management Specialist Group** holds a variety of talks, conferences and meetings on Configuration Management (including building and releasing software). It is well worth attending some of these events if you are based in or travelling around Europe.

www.stickyminds.com

StickyMinds.com is a portal for software development but has some good, original articles and technical papers from industry experts on the build process. StickyMinds.com is the online companion to Better Software magazine.

www-128.ibm.com/developerworks

IBM developerWorks is the portal for IBM's developer community. Although it focuses on IBM's software tool it also has sections dedicated to open source, Java and Linux – where you can usually find some good technical articles about the build process.

Selecting a Build Control Tool

This chapter attempts to summarize a basic set of requirements that any build control tool should fulfil in order to satisfy the requirements of a generic build process.

Process agnostic

There are many different software development methods: traditional Enterprise, open source, Agile and so on, and they all require distinct implementations of a build process. For example, Agile projects implementing Continuous Integration will require a tool that can support the building of software many times a day based on the set of atomic changes committed to a source code repository. However, traditional Enterprise projects might only require capabilities to carry out a Daily Build and Smoke Test. A build control tool should not force you down a particular process route. It should be open and adaptable to your own process.

Build Scripting tool agnostic

As I have discussed in this book, there are many build scripting tools and I'm sure new ones will be developed. Your build control tool should not impose which build scripting tool should be used. It should support all current build scripting tools that you use as well as have a basic capability for executing tools from the command line. This is so that new tools can be executed before a full integration is developed by the vendor or community.

Extendable version control integration

A build control tool should not force you to use any specific version control tool. It should work with your selected tool - as most do these days. However, its integration to your chosen tool should be open so that you can change the integration if you require. For example, you do not want the build control dictating when and how a baseline should be applied.

Basic IDE integration

There are some developers that hate IDEs and some that couldn't develop without them. If your development team do use an IDE then the build control tool should integrate with in someway. At the very least you should be notified of build success or failure from within your IDE. However, other nice-to-have capabilities include being able to execute a build (using the build control tools infrastructure) directly from the IDE and creating or editing the build control process flow.

Enforceable security

Once of the main functions of a build control tool is managing user access and permissions. For example, you might only want Build Engineers to be able to execute a Release Build process. However, all developers could execute an Integration Build. Similarly, you might want to store build results and only allow certain users to delete them. Your build control tool should therefore allow different users and users groups to be defined and then assigned to different capabilities, e.g., only Build Engineers can create a new Release Build.

Configurable reporting and metrics

In chapter 6 I discussed why I believe capturing and reporting on Build Metrics is so important. Obviously, if a build control tool can automatically capture a canned set of metrics for you then this is a great start. However, the build control tool should not confine you to these metrics; it should also allow you to define others to be captured and reported on, maybe by plugging in external scripts. Reports out of the build control tool, such as release notes, Bill of Material reports and so on should also be available but configurable so that you can include the information that you wish to see in them.

Build distribution

For build processes that require a significant time to build, the build control tool should provide some form of build distribution. This usually includes the installation of a number of dedicated build servers as a build server farm. The build control tool can then distribute a long running build to these servers depending on server load. It is useful if the build control tool collates a manifest of each of the build servers so that it can send an appropriate job to them, for example a Windows compilation job is only sent to a Windows server – not a Linux server.

APPENDIX B

Example Build Management Plan

Build Management Plan for *myReserve*

1. Introduction

1.1 Scope

The purpose of this document is to define the Build Management procedures to be followed by the *myReserve* project – an open source hotel reservation system (http://myreserve.sourceforge.net).

Note, this document is intended as a working "example" of a Build Management Plan. Although the project it is defined for uses open source rather than commercial build and deployment tools, the template itself can be tailored and applied to any development project. For example, if commercial build and deployment tools were being using in a complex business environment, then there should be more detail included on the integration of build and deployment into the corporate environment and the implementation of build and deployment security.

1.2 Definitions

All definitions are taken from *The Buildmeister's Guide* [BMG] Glossary.

1.3 References

- [SCM] *myReserve Software Configuration Management Plan.*
- [BMG] *The Buildmeister's Guide*, Second Edition, Buildmeister Books.

2. Build Management

2.1 Organization, Responsibilities, and Interfaces

The organizational structure of relevant roles to Build Management is illustrated in Figure 23.

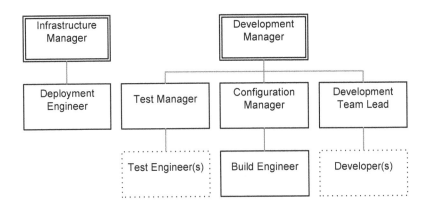

Figure 23 – *myReserve* organization chart

The **Build Engineer** will be responsible for:

- defining the project's build process based on the input of the **Developers**

- implementing, automating and securing the build process

- liaising with the **Configuration Manager** to ensure that the build process correctly interfaces to the SCM environment.

- automating or initiating the deployment of the application to Development and Acceptance Test environments.

The **Deployment Engineer** will be responsible for automating or initiating the deployment of the application to Production Environment.

2.2 Environment and Infrastructure

The infrastructure that is to be used for supporting the build and deployment process is illustrated in Figure 24. In more detail this infrastructure is utilized as follows:

The *myReserve* build scripts will be version controlled alongside the project source code on the **Version Control Server** (see the SCM plan [SCM] for more details). Development Integration builds will be automatically executed on the **Build Server** and deployed to a local instance of Apache Geronimo for Functional Integration Testing.

The outputs of each successful Integration build will be stored on the **Staging Server** (in this case a file system share on the Build Server).

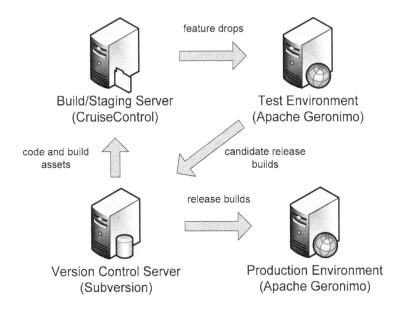

Figure 24 – *myReserve* **build and deployment infrastructure**

Approximately once a week, Feature Drops (Integration builds with specific, testable content) will be deployed by the Build Engineer into the **Test Environment** for validation by the Acceptance Testing team. Validated builds will then be securely stored back on the Version Control Server as candidate release builds.

The Deployment Engineer will deploy these builds from the Version Control Server into the secure **Production Environment** as and when required.

2.3 Tools

The following tools will be used to implement the build and deployment process:

- **Apache Ant** - for automating the compilation, unit testing and deployment processes.

- **CruiseControl** - to automate the execution of the Ant build scripts when developer changes are committed to the Version Control Server as well as to initiate deployment of Feature Drops to the Test Environment

- **Apache Geronimo** scripting - for automating the provisioning of servers, deployment of release builds and validation of their success on to the Production Environment.

A number of additional, related tools will be used to enforce and assess the quality of the input and output of the build process, including **JUnit**, **PMD** and **Fitnesse**.

3. Build Management Activities

3.1 Build Identification

3.1.1 Build Frequency

Two levels of Integration Build will be carried out as follows:

- **Partial Integration Build** - conforming to the Continuous Integration pattern - carried out automatically on each developer commit. This build will perform full static analysis of the application code base, compile the application and run through a defined subset of critical unit-tests.

- **Full Integration Build** - conforming to the Daily Build and Smoke Test - carried out automatically over night. This will perform full static analysis, compilation, full unit testing and deployment of the application to the development test instance. A small subset of automated functional tests will also be executed on the deployed application for Functional Integration Testing.

3.1.2 Build Identification

The outputs of each build will be labeled with the release number and unique build number in the form:

```
filename_REL-BLD.extension.
```

For example if the release number is 1.1 and the build number is 005, for a Web Application Archive this would result in a file named myReserveWeb_1.1-005.war. Note, that the Subversion global revision number[1] will also be recorded against the build in CruiseControl so that the build can be reconstructed at a later date.

Any Feature Drop builds which have been deployed and successfully validated in the Test Environment will be treated as candidate release builds and the outputs stored in a specific Subversion "release" repository. This repository will also be populated with release specific documentation (see 3.1.3 below).

Build automation projects defined in CruiseControl will conform to the following convention:

- Partial Integration Build projects will be named myReserve_REL_dev.
- Full Integration Build projects will be named myReserve_REL_int.
- Deployment (to Test) projects will be named myReserve_REL_deploy.

Where REL is the targeted release number, e.g. 1.1

---

[1] http://svnbook.red-bean.com/nightly/en/svn.basic.in-action.html

3.1.3 Build Directory Structure

The build and deployment directory structure for *myReserve* is illustrated Figure 25.

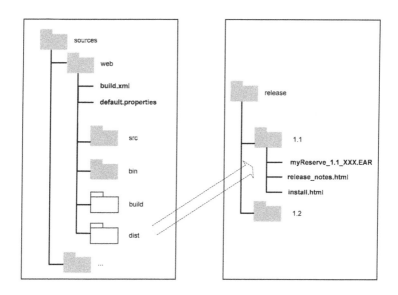

Figure 25 – *myReserve* build and deployment directory structure

Where the contents of this diagram are as follows:

- `build.xml` - Ant build script(s) for building the application
- `default.properties` - Ant build properties
- `src` - Java and HTML source code for the application
- `bin` – Apache Gernonimo deployment scripts for the application
- `release_notes.html` - description of the changes (new features, defects addressed) in the release of

the application

- `install.html` - instructions on how to install the application

Note that as the application contains multiple components there will be multiple directories in the `sources` repository with similar structures.

3.1.5 Build Workspaces

The Partial Integration Build will use and update a single Subversion workspace (working directory). To ensure a clean and repeatable build process, the Full Integration Build will create and populate a new Subversion workspace. A file system directory will be created on the Build Server to hold CruiseControl build results and build outputs.

3.2 Build Control

3.2.1 Security and Authorization

The following security restrictions will be implemented on the project:

- **Any user** will have permission to update the Apache Ant build scripts and CruiseControl projects, however because of availability and experience it is expected that the Build Engineer will carry out these changes.
- The **Build Engineer** role will be the only role authorized to deploy to the **Test Environment**.
- The **Build Engineer** role is the only role authorized to commit a validated release candidate build to the Version Control Server.
- The **Build Engineer** role is the only role authorized to update and version the release documentation.
- The **Deployment Engineer** role will be the only

role authorized to provision and deploy to the **Production Environment**.

Where authorization is required this will be enabled by user login and password mechanisms.

3.2.2 Integration to Configuration and Change Control

See the SCM plan [SCM] for more details on how the build and deployment process is integrated to Change Control.

4 Build Status Accounting

4.1 Project Media Storage

All Integrations builds are transient are not expected to be backed up. All candidate release builds will be backed up with the Subversion repository - see the SCM plan [SCM] for more details.

4.2 Release Process

The release process for *myReserve* is illustrated in Figure 26.

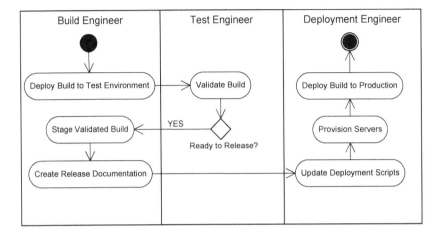

Figure 26 – *myReserve* release process

In more detail these steps are describe in Table 3.

Role	Activities	Description
Build Engineer	Deploy Build to Test Environment	A Feature Drop is chosen as suitable for Acceptance Testing. The Build Engineer deploys this build from the Staging Server into the Test Environment.
Build Engineer	Stage Validated Build	If the Feature Drop passes all Acceptance Tests and is validated as "ready to release" then the Build Engineer stages the build into the Subversion release repository.
Build Engineer	Create Release Documentation	The Build Engineer creates the release documentation for the build (including release note and installation instructions) and versions them alongside the staged build.

Deployment Engineer	Update Deployment Scripts	Using the content of the release documentation, the Deployment Engineer creates or updates the automated deployment scripts.
Deployment Engineer	Provision Servers	The Deployment Engineer makes sure that the appropriate Production servers have been provisioned and are available.
Deployment Engineer	Deploy Build to Production	The Deployment Engineer deploys the build into the Production Environment.

Table 3 – *myReserve* release process steps

4.3 Reports and Audits

An overview of activities for monitoring and reporting on the build and deployment process are described in

Role	Activities	Description
Automated	Report on Integration Build results	The results of each Integration Build will be automatically recorded in CruiseControl.
Automated / Build Engineer	Report on Feature Drop content	The incremental features that have been developed and are available for Acceptance testing will be retrieved and documented.
Test Engineer	Report on Build Validation	The Test Engineer will document the results of the Acceptance Testing for the build.
Build Engineer	Report on Release content (Bill of Materials).	The Build Engineer will create a Bill of Materials, detailing the content of the release, including features, bug-fixes and installation steps. As defined in 4.2 above.

Deployment Engineer	Report on Production Deployment	The results of the deployment to Production as well as the exact configuration of the environment will be documented by the Deployment Engineer.

Table 4 – *myReserve* reporting activities

4.4 Milestones

Milestones are described in the project's Microsoft Project Plan.

5. Training and Resources

The training courses recommended by role are listed in Table 5.

Courses	Roles
Essentials of Apache Ant	Build Engineer
	Deployment Engineer
Apache Geronimo Application Server Administration	Build Engineer
	Deployment Engineer

Table 5 – Recommended training courses

6. Subcontractor and Vendor Software Control

myReserve does not currently subcontract software development. However, they do incorporate open-source products into their systems which must be carefully controlled. The versions of all of these products as well as the tools used in the Development, Acceptance

Test and Production Environment's (including Apache Ant, CruiseControl and so on) are recorded in the SCM plan [SCM].

Appendix A - Administration Procedures

Issues to be covered include:

- How to reuse Ant common targets when a new project component is developed.
- Support and maintenance of Apache Geronimo application server environments.
- Archiving and maintenance of CruiseControl projects and build results.

The backup and recovery of Subversion repositories is detailed in the SCM plan [SCM].

Glossary

Active Development Line

A project's integration branch containing the latest development baseline. The Active Development Line is accessed via an individual private workspace for day-to-day development and integration.

active object

A build derived object that has not or is yet to be staged, such an object is view private rather than under version control.

agile development

An umbrella term for individual software development methodologies such as Crystal methods, eXtreme Programming, and feature-driven development. Agile development methods emphasize customer satisfaction through continuous delivery of functional software. Although similar to iterative development, agile development methods typically promote less rigorous process enforcement.

Agile Software Delivery

An end to end software delivery process with continual builds and deployments. Agile Software Delivery aims to reduce the risk of delayed integration and deployment by building early and reusing previously build objects.

Application Lifecycle Management

The management and control of all application-related information over an entire life cycle. It incorporates a continuously repeating cycle of inter-related steps such as: definition, design, development, testing and deployment.

artifact

A piece of information that is produced, modified, or used by a process, defines an area of responsibility, and is subject to version control.

baseline

A metadata object that typically represents a stable configuration across a collection of artifacts.

bill of materials

The Bill of Materials lists the constituent parts of a given version of a product or application, and where the physical parts may be found. It describes the changes made in the version and refers to how the product may be installed.

branch

An object that specifies a linear sequence of element versions.

branching strategy

A strategy for isolation and integration of changes on a software project through the use of branches. A branching strategy defines the types of branches you use, how these branches relate to one another, and how you move changes between branches.

build

An operational version of a system or part of a system that demonstrates a subset of the capabilities to be provided in the final product.

build auditing

The process of recording which files and directories (and which versions of them) are read or written by the operating system during the course of a build.

build avoidance

The capability of a build program to fulfil a build request using an existing object, rather than creating a new derived object for the specific build step.

build distribution

The process of distributing the build process across a number of servers or computer processes so as to shorten the total build time.

build management

The identification and definition of what to build, the execution of the build process, and the reporting of its results. Build management capabilities also include build auditing, build avoidance and build distribution.

build pipeline

A "pipeline" of related build processes that get executed on the successful completion of each other. A build pipeline is usually implemented using staged objects.

build server farm

A collection of virtual of physical hardware used to reduce total build times or share infrastructure across a number of projects.

change request

A general term for any request from a stakeholder to change an artifact or process. Documented in the change request is information on the origin and impact of the current problem, the proposed solution, and its cost.

classpath

An environmental variable or build file setting which tells the JVM where to look for Java programs. The entries in a classpath should contain either directories or jar files.

clearmake

A make-compatible build tool that is part of the IBM Rational ClearCase product and that provides build audit and build avoidance features.

CMMI

The Capability Maturity Model Integration (CMM) is a method for evaluating the maturity of organisations. The CMMI was developed by the Software Engineering Institute (SEI) at Carnegie Mellon University.

component

A metadata object that groups a set of related directory and file elements within a project.

continuous integration

The process of frequently integrating individual developer's changes into a product's integration environment. Continuous Integration normally necessitates a fully automated and reproducible build, including testing, that runs many times a day. This allows each developer to integrate daily thus reducing integration problems.

continuous staging

The process of accumulating the output of multiple continuous integration builds into a staging area and automatically executing a system build.

deployment

The act of moving staged or packaged artifacts to other systems for further testing or release.

deployment component

A built object or executable such as a .jar, .dll or .exe file that is part of the complete product or application.

deployment unit

A self-contained, installable, documented and traceable release of a software product or application. The deployment unit includes the contents of a product's release build, its bill of materials and any other supporting artefacts.

EAR

A Java Enterprise ARchive file is an archive (like a JAR file) containing Java class files and supporting artifacts (such as images). EAR files are used to package J2EE applications for deployment. J2EE files containing additional required files above and beyond JAR files that define the environment in which they are to be deployed and executed.

feature drop

An installable and testable build that contains an incremental subset of the applications features. Feature Drops are typically created to allow (non-developer) Acceptance Testing to take place.

golden master

A final software release that is used to produce distribution media for customers or end-users.

integration

The process of bringing together independently developed changes to form a testable piece of software. Integration can occur at many levels, eventually culminating in a complete software system.

integration build

A build that is carried out by an assigned integrator or central function to assess the effect of integrating a set of changes across a development team. This type of build can be carried out manually be a lead developer or a member of the build team, or alternately via an automatically scheduled program or service.

J2EE

Java 2 Platform, Enterprise Edition is an environment for developing and deploying enterprise applications. Defined by Sun Microsystems Inc., the J2EE platform consists of a set of services, application programming interfaces (APIs), and protocols that provide the functionality for developing multitiered, Web-based applications.

JAR

A Java ARchive file is an archive (like a ZIP file) containing Java class files and supporting artifacts (such as images). JAR files are used to package Java applications for deployment.

JDK

A Java Development Kit is a software development package from Sun Microsystems that implements the basic set of tools needed to write, test and debug Java applications and applets

JRE

A Java Runtime Environment consists of the JVM, the Java platform core classes, and supporting files. It is the runtime part of the JDK and does not include a compiler, debugger, or supporting tools.

JVM

A Java Virtual Machine is a virtual machine that runs Java byte code generated by Java compilers.

makefile

A makefile details the files, dependencies, and rules by which an executable application is built. Makefiles are executed using the make program.

managed code

Executable code that is managed by its targeted execution framework. Managed code is Microsoft's definition for the output of languages that run on its .NET platform.

milestone integration

The process of integrating code basis at a specific project milestone, e.g. once a month. Also called big-bang integration.

mock object

A simulated code object, for example a class to mimic a database if the actual database is not available.

Private Workspace

An isolated environment where developers can control the versions of code that they are working on.

Promotion Line

A branch created for a distinct level of assembly or integration, i.e. for integrating the components of a system or for allowing a site to integrate before executing a remote delivery.

private build

A build that is carried out by a developer in their own workspace. This type of build is usually created for the purpose of checking the ongoing status of the developer's changes.

release

A release is a stable, executable version of a product. An internal release is used only by the development organization, as part of a milestone, or for a demonstrations to users or customers. An external release is delivered to end users.

release build

A build that is carried out by a central function, usually a member of the build team. This build is created with the express intention of being delivered to a customer – either internal or external. A release build is also usually created in an isolated and controlled environment.

release management

The packaging and authorization of a release build so as to enable its deployment to a test or live environment. Release management can also involves the creation of a deployment unit for deploying a partial or multiple products releases.

release package

The packaging of a release build into a form so that it is readily installable and deployable.

Release–Prep Line

A branch created for the purposes of conducting or stabilizing a release (whilst also allowing delivery to the Active Development Line to continue).

RSS

RSS is a family of XML formats for syndicating information across the Internet. Rather confusingly, the abbreviation can be used to refer to a number of standards or versions of RSS as follows: Rich Site Summary (RSS 0.91), RDF Site Summary (RSS 0.9 and 1.0) or Really Simple Syndication (RSS 2.0). The technology behind RSS allows you to subscribe to websites that have provided RSS feeds; these are typically sites that change or add content regularly. To subscribe you typically use a feed reader or aggregator.

Software Configuration Management

A software-engineering discipline that comprises the tools and techniques (processes or methodology) a company uses to manage change to its software assets. Software Configuration Management typically includes Version Management, Change Management, Build Management and Process Management capabilities.

SSH

Secure SHell is a command interface and protocol for securely accessing remote computers.

staged integration

The process of integrating a collective set of changes in isolation (usually on a branch) before integrating them back onto the mainline. Staged integration is a practical form of integration where it is not possible to "pollute" the mainline, for example to carry out a critical maintence fix.

staged object

An active object that has been placed under version control.

staging

The process of putting active object files under version control.

variant

An individual source code item, product or application that has been tailored for a specific customer or environment. For example, a commercial application can be developed in parallel for multiple operating system variants such Microsoft Windows, UNIX and Linux.

version control

A subset of software configuration management that deals with tracking version evolution of a file or directory.

WAR

A Java Web ARchive file is an archive (like a JAR file) containing Java class files and supporting artifacts (such as images). WAR files are used to package Web-based Java applications for deployment. WAR files containing additional required files above and beyond JAR files that define the environment in which they are to be deployed and executed.

Wiki

A wiki is a software system that allows users to create, edit, and link web pages easily. Wiki's are installed on a web server machine and accessed and updated by Internet browsers.

work product component

A source code, configuration, or documentation file that is part of your product and is changed as part of a change request. Work product components are usually grouped together to form some type of deployment component.

workspace

A generic term for an operating system directory structure created from a specific configuration out of a version control tool.

ZIP

ZIP is a popular data compression format. Files that have been compressed with the ZIP format are called ZIP files and usually end with a .zip extension.

Table of Figures

Bibliography

[AgileM01] Cunnigham, Ward, et al. *Manifesto for Agile Development.* http://agilemanifesto.org/

[Berczuk02] Berczuk, Stephen and Appleton, Brad. *Software Configuration Management Patterns: Effective Teamwork, Practical Integration.* Addison-Wesley, 2002.

[BerczukBM] Berczuk, Appleton, Konieczka. *Build Management for an Agile Team.* www.cmcrossroads.com/articles/agileoct03.pdf

[Dalgarno07] Dalgarno, Mark and Beuche Danillo. *Variant Management.* www.bcs-cmsg.org.uk/conference/2007/papers/dalgarno.pdf.

[FowlerCI] Fowler, Foemmel. *Continuous Integration.* www.martinfowler.com/articles/continuousIntegration.html

[Friedl06] Friedl, Jeffrey. *Mastering Regular Expressions.* O'Reilly 2006.

[Hatcher02] Hatcher, Erik and Loughran, Steve. *Java Development with Ant.* Greenwich, Conn. Pearson Education, 2002.

[Hunter04] Hunter, David, et al. *Beginning XML (Programmer to Programmer)*, Third Edition. Wiley, 2004.

[Lee06] Lee, Kevin. *IBM Rational ClearCase, Ant and CruiseControl: The Java Developer's Guide to Accelerating and Automating the Build Process.* IBM Press, 2006.

[LeeABM07] Lee, Kevin. *Apache Ant – The Buildmeister's Guide*. Buildmeister Books, 2007.

[Loughran07] Loughran, Steve and Hatcher, Erik. *Ant in Action*. Manning, 2007.

[McConnell96] McConnell, Steve. *IEEE Software Best Practice: Daily Build and Smoke Test*. IEEE Software, Vol. 13, No. 4, July 1996.

[Schwartz01] Schwartz, Randall, et al.. *Learning Perl*, 4th Edition. O'Reilly, 2005.

[Stubllebine03] Stubblebine, Tony. *Regular Expression Pocket Reference*. O'Reilly, 2003

[Spencer92] Spencer, Henry. *#ifdef Considered Harmful, or Portability Experience with C News*. www.chris-lott.org/resources/cstyle/ifdefs.pdf.

[Sukanen04] Sukanen, Jari. *Extension Framework for Symbian OS applications*. www.tml.tkk.fi/Publications/Thesis/sukanen.pdf.

[Wagner02] Wagner, Richard. *XSLT for Dummies*. For Dummies, 2002.

Index